BLIND SPOTS
AND WRINKLES

Blind Spots and Wrinkles

UNDERSTANDING OUR BLIND SPOTS AND BEHAVIOR QUIRKS

Deborah D. Delbridge

CovenantBridge Publishing

Blind Spots and Wrinkles by Deborah D. Delbridge
Published by CovenantBridge Publishing

CovenantBridge
P u b l i s h i n g

Author Website: www.DeborahDelbridge.com

First Printing, 2022

Unless otherwise noted, all Scripture quotations are from the New King James Version of the Bible. Copyright 1982 by Thomas Nelson, Inc., publishers. Used by permission.

Proof reading by: Carol Davis

ISBN: 9798986218304

Contents

Forewords

Blind Spots and Wrinkles is full of interesting observations that will provide the readers with several *Aw-hah moments* as the readers discover the origins of common behaviors and motives. The content of this book offers the readers a pathway to becoming more self-aware of their behavior and their emotional rationalizations.

As a licensed psychologist, I have counseled people that were immersed in pride, fear, unforgiveness, and jealousy and I have seen the damage that those wrong mind-sets have caused. Debbie's new book is a practical *How To* book on getting rid of those self-destructive behavior patterns.

Blind Spots and Wrinkles blends Christian teaching with psychological principles in a harmonious way. I would highly recommend this book to my Christian clients.

Dr. Jeff Walker, Licensed Clinical Psychologist, specializing in Christian counseling. Dr. Jeff has more than 30 years of pastoral experience and 20 years as a Law Enforcement Chaplain.

www.DrJeffWalker.com

As a church revival historian, I recognize that humility and repentance are necessary elements for revival to happen. Debbie's new book teaches on pride and the other hidden iniquities that keep Christians bound to their Adamic nature and hamper their ability to walk consistently in the spirit. Traditionally, Pentecostal Christians focus on the gifts of the spirit and often overlook the fruit of the spirit. It would be difficult for a believer to have love, joy, peace, long-suffering, kindness, goodness, faithfulness, gentleness, and self-control if they have a raging stronghold of jealousy consuming them. This book teaches how to uproot jealousy and the other soul strongholds that limit spiritual maturity. Debbie teaches on the origins of wrong motives that drive wrong attitudes and actions.

I have known Debbie for almost 30 years. I whole-heartedly endorse this book. I believe *Blind Spots and Wrinkles* and teachings like it are needed in the church today. This book is about sanctification which is essential to operate in unobstructed obedience to God. Too many Christians have wrong motives that muddy the waters of what God is wanting to do. We must prepare our hearts so we can cooperate with what God is wanting to do in this season.

Dr. Roberts Liardon, Pastor, Church Historian, Renown Revival Expert and Author (written more than 80 books including the "God's Generals" series, sold over 16 million copies). He has ministered in 127 nations and is the founder of Embassy Global Network.

www.RobertsLiardon.org

One

Blind Spots

What is a blind spot? In driving, it can refer to a section of the road which the driver can't see because their view is blocked by their own vehicle. However, in psychological terms, a blind spot is an area where a person's view of reality is obstructed by their own pride, fear, or willful ignorance. It can be an area where we respond in denial because of our lack of understanding of the matter or because our prejudices and preconceptions block our view of a situation. So rather than attempt to understand different truths, people, as a rule, just live in denial on matters that they don't want to deal with.

We live in a society that embraces blind spots. Daytime talk shows propagate the concept of *my truth*. When Oprah had her show, they celebrated the concept of *owning your own truth*. Many people still ascribe to the *my truth* notion.

However, there is a backlash, and some sectors are calling it what it is. The Urban Dictionary says, *my truth* is a "pretentious substitute for 'non-negotiable personal opinion.' Often used by academics, this is a controversial phrase for avoiding arguments because people can contradict your opinion but not your 'truth.' The phrase is often used when seeking to justify a controversial stance or action because people are not allowed to argue with 'your truth.'"

Sadly, most people still wholeheartedly embrace the concept of *my truth* although they may not label it as that. Most people believe that their version of reality is absolute truth and others are simply wrong if they don't view people and situations through the same filtered lenses and biases as them. Most people don't want to be controversial so they have learned to keep silent about certain issues around those that would challenge their questionable opinions. But, in the privacy of their own minds, they fully embrace their opinions as absolute truth.

There is a psychological principle that you will hear repeatedly throughout this book and that is – *our beliefs and behaviors are driven from our subconscious mind and not our conscious mind.* Biases are rooted in our subconscious mind, so our version of reality isn't the full reality of a specific situation. Situations, like people, are like diamonds, in that they are multi-faceted. There are several sides, facets, factors, and influences in any given incident, circumstance, or event.

We are not God. We are not all-knowing. Yet, we form an opinion that gets imbedded in our belief system, and it becomes extremely difficult to change our views once they have been established. Oftentimes, we are only able to see one side of an issue, and we won't allow ourselves to see other facets because we have already established an opinion on the matter. We may overemphasize one facet of the situation and make it so huge in our mind's eye, that we are incapable of seeing any other perspective on the issue.

Our beliefs get woven into a tapestry in our subconscious mind, often getting interwoven with similar beliefs. Our subconscious mind knows just where to fit a new piece of the puzzle (new information) into our subconscious network of beliefs. We unknowingly categorize people and situations. And we oftentimes, don't allow ourselves to view a situation from a different angle because that would distort how we have initially labeled it subconsciously.

This book will delve into how our beliefs and behaviors get established and will explore how we all have weaknesses in our subconscious mind that influence and direct our behavior. However, before we dive deeper into those areas, I believe it is important to first understand how information is received. If we are unwilling to admit that there may be areas in our subconscious mind that are self-sabotaging or even sinful, then reading this book won't be helpful. All of us need to allow the Holy Spirit to highlight areas that may need improvement within ourselves.

Iniquities within ourselves must be acknowledged before we can uproot them. Understanding how blind spots can happen is really the first step in *peeling the onion* of human behavior and becoming more self-aware. There is a necessity now, more than ever, to stop living with our *head in the sand*. We, as a people, need to break the habit of ignoring or denying information just because it doesn't fit comfortably within the borders of our comfort zones.

Psychology tells us that 10% of our mind is conscious, and the other 90% is subconscious. We don't know if those percentages are accurate, but let's assume they are for the purpose of this illustration. Imagine if there were a bucket of rocks and water filled up to the 90% marker which represents our subconscious mind. If we were to place a large new rock into the bucket, that large rock wouldn't sink down below the water line because there is no room for it. The only way that new rock would get immersed would be if the rocks were rearranged and an existing large rock were removed to make room for it.

That is an illustration of how our belief system works. Our belief system is rooted in our subconscious mind. In order for new information (the large new rock) to be accepted and believed in our subconscious mind, we would have to remove a belief we have already embraced, and most people just aren't willing to do that. So often, it may not matter how factual and verifiable the new information is. Most people won't be willing to accept and believe it if it requires that they draw out a belief that they already have. Small bits of information, details that are represented by little pebbles, may be received and believed if they can fit correctly into our current belief system. However, if we hear a statement that contradicts our beliefs, human nature wants to automatically reject it because it doesn't line up with our current rocks. When we automatically reject information just because it doesn't fit into our rock collection, that area can become a blind spot.

This is a very important concept to understand because our bucket of rocks (our gut, our subconscious mind) affects everything. It affects our salvation, our faith for promises, our identity, our self-esteem, our success level in life, and our relationship with God and man. Our bucket of rocks can and does prevent us from recognizing truth.

In the first paragraph, I mentioned that just like we can have blinds when we drive, we can also have psychological blind spots. Psychological blind spots can manifest when a person's view of reality is obstructed by their own pride, fear, or willful ignorance. I will address each one of these blind spot causes.

Pride

Let's look at the bucket of rocks and water analogy once again. Oftentimes, when someone has a lot of pride and a new rock (new information) is tossed into the bucket, that new rock may bounce out and not land in the bucket. Whereas someone with a minimal amount of pride, may allow that rock to sit on top of the existing rocks and water line for a while. What do I mean by this? I mean people that aren't prideful won't be quick to reject new information. They will allow the rock to sit in the bucket even if they don't embrace it as truth. They allow the new information to be acknowledged in their conscious mind as an interesting theory, but they neither accept nor reject it because they don't know if there is truth in the new information. In fact, oftentimes, new information has a mixture of both truth and falsity, so it shouldn't be wholly accepted or rejected right away. New information should be tempered and held in a holding pattern until (for a believer) the Holy Spirit brings revelation, wisdom, and clarity on the issue.

Pride is a big deal. Pride leads to deceptive thinking. Oftentimes, the more pride a person has, the more delusional they are. There are examples in the Bible and in modern times. For example, Daniel 4 tells us that King Nebuchadnezzar embraced pride and lost his mind for seven years. In modern times, both David Koresh and Jim Jones were preachers that started out with correct theology. However, their pride went unchecked, and they started to believe unscriptural things. As a result, they created their own false doctrines. Their pride led to deceptive thinking and soon they were leaders of cults, which caused the deaths of hundreds of people.

A root of pride in someone's subconscious mind can give them a cold heart. Ezekiel 11:19 and 36:26 both talk about God removing our "heart of stone" and giving us a heart of flesh. Our hearts can get hard because of man's sinful nature. Pride was sired into mankind at the fall in the Garden of Eden, and that pride can make our hearts hard and cold towards God. Our heart can become like a frozen pond, hard and cold. If someone were to throw a stone at a frozen pond, most likely that rock would bounce a few times, but it wouldn't crack the ice. The same is true with new information to a person with excessive pride. A prideful person thinks they know everything they need to know in order to form opinions. Whether they verbalize it or not, they believe there isn't anything a peer or subordinate can say to them that would be beneficial to them. A prideful person believes their version of the truth is the real truth, and if anyone disagrees with them, then they are wrong. Pride blinds a person so they can't see their own self-deception.

Pride is the reason many people haven't accepted the salvation message. They can't accept Christ into their heart because there is a fortress of pride, a barrier of ice, stopping them. The gospel message of salvation is available to all. It simply takes confessing with your mouth and believing in your heart that Jesus is Lord. Well, believing doesn't happen in our conscious mind; believing happens in our subconscious mind. Unless there is a crack in the ice of their heart, the gospel message won't sink down into their belief system.

The reason a high percentage of people find God when they go through a crisis is the situation humbled them. When a person is in trouble and facing circumstances they can't fix, they recognize that they need God. It is in those seasons when the heart is humble, that the ice can crack and allow an agreeable concept to go from the conscious mind to the subconscious mind, where it becomes a legitimate belief.

In order for us to see our blind spots, we must be willing to crack the ice of our pride. We must be willing to examine some of the rocks in our bucket. I am not just talking about spiritual beliefs, I am talking about every day, normal beliefs we have that we have developed over the years. For example, if new information came out that proved your favorite actor was a terrible person – you wouldn't believe it. That actor may have been characterized as a hero in every movie he has been in and as such, we have formed our opinion of him as a hero. Our belief system can be so fortified that we wouldn't consider the new information even with verifiable evidence. Regardless of the type or amount of evidence, it wouldn't be believed because the rock in our bucket (that actor) has identified him as good. It would be too hard to dig down and grab that rock and replace it. Do we know that actor personally? No. We have no idea what he is like when the camera isn't rolling. But we, like millions of others, have been conditioned to believe he a good person.

The same can be true in reverse. Our favorite news network may have spent years indoctrinating us in subtle and/or overt ways that certain politicians and world leaders are bad. We may have embraced the narrative we were fed, and we may have grown to hate a public figure even though it had all been propaganda. We then hear information that the leader is good after all, but our belief system won't allow that new information to be embraced as truth. There may be undeniable evidence of their great accomplishments, but in our mind, that person will forever be a villain. Again, it is the same thing. We are unwilling to allow our opinions about people and situations to be changed because our pride has already judged and categorized them in our rock collection (our subconscious belief system).

Pride blinds us and it causes us to categorize people and situations as either positive or negative, so they fit into our rock pile the way we want them to. However, the truth is, most people and most situations have both positive and negative aspects to them, so we need to learn to re-sort our rocks when we gain a new understanding of something.

God wants to help us in the areas that we don't see clearly. But as Christians, we won't be able to recognize truth if we don't actively work on rooting out pride. All of us, in this season, need to take measures to recognize pride in our lives.

Fear

Just like pride creates blind spots, fear can as well. Fear can cause a person's fragile psyche to refuse to see truth and an auto response of denial kicks in. This type of denial isn't just a person metaphorically holding their fingers in their ears and humming. That kind of denial describes a person who is fully aware of a situation, but they are choosing to ignore it. The denial I am talking about is where there isn't a conscious decision to ignore it. It isn't a subject they have weighed out and thought through. Their denial is an emotional defense mechanism that the brain does automatically because dealing with the reality of a situation would be too difficult.

Here are a couple scenarios that illustrate this type of fear-based blind spot:

Example #1:
Over the years, I have known of several cases where young girls had been molested by their father, stepfather, mother's boyfriend, or uncle. When the mother of the girl was asked why she didn't stop it, the mother usually said she wasn't aware of it.

How could a mother not know that her own daughter was being sexually abused? There would be clues, expressions, and demeanors from both the victim and the abuser. The mother should have sensed that something wasn't right.

How could a woman embrace denial when her own child was being hurt physically and emotionally? Maybe the abuser was manipulative and controlling and through years of dominance, he had taught her not to question anything he does. Perhaps she had learned to turn a blind eye to all her suspicions. Maybe she feared confrontation, so she followed the path she had learned to follow – simple compliance. Or perhaps the man provided security and financial stability and her fear of homelessness overrode any domestic awkwardness. That fear can create a blind spot where the mother genuinely won't let herself believe her daughter is being molested.

Example #2

I have known a few men that have fallen into this next scenario. These men felt lonely and amorous, so they responded to good looking women that reached out to them either online or in person. The men responded out of curiosity and, quite frankly, their pent-up lust. Over time, the men built friendships with the women. The women were available, subservient, and affectionate towards them. As a result, they made the men feel good about themselves. The issue was these women were scammers. They always had financial needs, sometimes real and sometimes fabricated. They gave the men affection, attention, and emotional support in exchange for money. These lonely men allowed these women to become their whole world to the point that they were faithful to only them. However, the women had other men that they were stringing along and scamming as well. Friends and family tried to warn the men about being a *sugar daddy* or *meal ticket* to these women, but they couldn't see it and didn't want to believe it. The men dismissed their friends' labels because, in their minds, those friends just didn't understand the dynamics of those relationships.

Were my male friends being used for their money? Absolutely. But they didn't want to see that truth because if they recognized it, then they would have to make some hard decisions. They would be forced to end those relationships, and they just weren't emotionally ready to do that. Those women were filling a gap of loneliness in those men, so they were willing to live in denial. The emotional defense mechanism of denial allowed them to live in that false existence, rather than face the harsh reality of loneliness. Fear of being alone caused those men to ignore the fact that they were being used.

Willful Ignorance

Willful ignorance is a little tougher to write about because it can affect the destination of where a person spends eternity. There are people that refuse to seek God because they are afraid of what may be revealed. I know a couple of people that have lost loved ones that have told me they want to spend eternity wherever their loved one resides. Even though they were curious about having a relationship with God, they didn't want to pursue it because they wanted to be with their deceased loved one. One of them even said she would feel like she was betraying to her husband if she "converted and got really religious." Some people don't investigate the scriptures because it is an easier reality to believe everyone goes to heaven. They don't want to be confronted with the reality of hell and the possibility that their loved one could be there.

There are other people who choose to remain ignorant about spiritual matters because they are secretly mad at God. They don't understand why a loved one had to die or why an accident occurred. They don't pursue God, and some have adopted an incorrect theology that says God owes them because He stole from them. They are clueless that God didn't cause the tragedy in their life, and it is the devil's objective to *"rob, steal, and destroy,"* as it says in John 10:10.

A while back, there was a woman at my place of employment that said an energy in the form of a white light showed up with her in her digital pictures. She said she thought it was her decreased grandfather. I offered to give her a copy of my book, "Real Stories of Angeles, Demons, and the Supernatural," so she could learn about supernatural entities. She declined. She said her grandmother always told her to avoid anything that talks about demons. From childhood, she was taught that ignorance is best when it comes to the demonic world. I understand the grandmother's instruction, which encouraged kids not to dabble with demonic forces. So, in that sense, it is true. But when it comes to spiritual knowledge, ignorance is not bliss. Hosea 4:6 says, *"My people perish for lack of knowledge."* So, while we absolutely shouldn't play around with witchcraft, we shouldn't be ignorant of the spirit world either.

I explained to my co-worker that demons thrive when two things are present – fear and ignorance. By gaining knowledge of the spirit world and understanding the spiritual authority we have through Christ, we can dispel both fear and ignorance. Demons will greatly reduce their activity in our lives if we are knowledgeable and fearless. Demons are like cockroaches. They get in our house and invade our kitchen when the lights are out. But as soon as someone comes in the kitchen and flips on the light, they scamper and flee. Well, when we recognize there is demonic activity in our life, and we shine the light on it, demons will try to run and hide. Fear and ignorance actually welcome demonic activity into our lives. Pretending they don't exist, just gives them permission to rob, steal, and destroy (John 10:10).

This last type of willful ignorance I want to address pertains to those propensities towards certain types of sin in our life. I realize *sin* is an undesirable word and the word *weakness* is more palatable. But the truth of the matter is, most of our weaknesses are sins regardless of the label we put on them.

We tend to think sin is always preceded by temptation. We assume we are faced with a decision to say "yes" or "no" to a sin. However, that usually isn't the case. Most of the time, sin is an auto response to a situation. For example, when asked a question we don't want to answer, we may lie. It wasn't a preplanned lie; it was a knee-jerk response because something within us didn't want to be honest in that moment. We fail to recognize that lying is one of the biggest manifestations of pride. But if we get away with our lie and we don't think it hurt anybody, we don't give it a second thought. We don't question the root cause of the lie, and we certainly don't confront the pride in our hearts.

We cannot be willfully ignorant anymore. Time is too short, and the mission ahead is too big to allow these hidden propensities towards certain types of sin to go unchecked. These autopilot areas of ugliness, these soul iniquities, need to be confronted, so we can allow Christ to shine through us.

Pride, fear, and willful ignorance all cause us to have blind spots where our version of reality isn't true. We don't want to believe a version that doesn't line up with our bucket of rocks, so we simply don't.

Cognitive Dissonance

Psychology has a term for what I have been describing in this chapter - it's *Cognitive Dissonance*. There are different definitions and schools of thought revolving around the Cognitive Dissonance Theory. However, a widely accepted characteristic of it is – a person can't accept evidence of something because the new evidence disagrees with what he or she already believes.

When we reject new information about something because it doesn't line up with what has already been established in our belief system, that area then becomes a blind spot to us. And I would theorize that the stronger our pride is, the stronger our cognitive dissonance will be.

I believe it is necessary for Christians to understand cognitive dissonance for two reasons:

1) It is needed, so we don't automatically reject information that may be true and factual.

2) We need to understand the concept, so we don't allow new factual information to shipwreck our faith. There are absolute truths in the Bible that we have embraced in our subconscious mind and that is good. However, there may be assumptions or incorrect details that we may have embraced that may not be accurate.

Sometimes we go through a shaking, and we are forced to confront our beliefs. Whenever I read the Hebrews 12:26-28 passage, I always think about this. The passage reads, *"Whose voice then shook the earth; but now He has promised, saying 'Yet once more I will shake not only the earth but heaven." Now this "Yet once more,' indicates the removal of those things that are being shaken, as of things that are made, that the things that cannot be shaken may remain. Therefore, since we are receiving a kingdom which cannot be shaken, let us have grace, by which we may serve God acceptably with reverence and godly fear."*

If we were to envision a mountain that goes through an earthquake, we would see that dirt and loose gravel would shake off and fall down the hill, but the solid rock would remain. The word of God is like the solid rock. It remains regardless of the shaking. If we have a promise from God, that word stands regardless of the circumstances around us. However, we may have assumptions that are like the gravel around the rock. When a shaking occurs, that loose gravel will fall away. We may see that some of the details about the promise were just assumptions and not part of the original word/rock that God gave us. This Hebrews passage tells us the *"things that are made"* fall away. Our assumptions or wrong conclusions are the man-made details, and they don't last after a shaking. They fall away like loose gravel; however, the firm foundation of the Word of God stands.

Perhaps a Bible teacher taught us end-time events incorrectly, so we have incorrect opinions on how events will play out. Maybe God gave us a promise, but we added our preferences or assumptions of how it would happen. Having our faith rocked with new information isn't necessarily a bad thing. It lets us separate the rock from the gravel to provide us with more clarity. However, some Christians can allow their faith to get shipwrecked because they thought some of the loose gravel of assumptions, which proved wrong, was part of the original rock (Word of God), so they abandon the Word. They threw the *baby out with the bath water* as the saying goes. They aborted the promise of God because they incorrectly assumed details that weren't part of the original word or promise.

Closing Thoughts

We can't afford to have these blind spots any longer. We need spiritual clarity now more than ever. We must be willing to dissect some of our beliefs and identify which beliefs are rocks and which ones are loose gravel. We must be willing to look at situations from different perspectives, so we can have a more accurate view of reality.

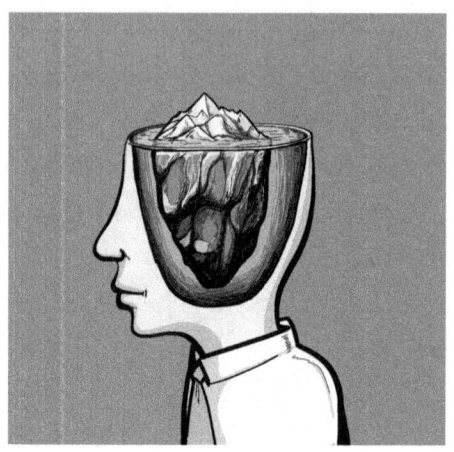

Two

Our Psyche

Before we delve into the hidden, subconscious iniquities that dwell within us, it is important to understand our human psyche. Understanding the components and characteristics of our conscious mind and subconscious mind is essential in ferreting out those ugly weaknesses that reside in us.

Most Christians would embrace the concept that mankind is a three-part being. We are a spirit. We have a soul. And we live in a body. That definition has been around for decades. Our soul contains our mind, will, emotions, intellect, memory, and creativity. And our spirit becomes the house where the Holy Spirit resides when we accept Jesus Christ as our savior and make Him Lord of our lives.

The phrase *subconscious mind* is a psychological term and isn't used very much in Christian teaching. Christians don't deny that the subconscious mind exists, they just haven't known how to define it since that term is not in the Bible. The Bible uses terms like *heart, mind, soul,* and *spirit* almost interchangeably, and it is up to reader to determine the context of what is being taught.

If we go back to that bucket of rocks illustration, imagine that the bucket now has a layer of sand at the very bottom. That layer of sand is our human spirit. It is the essence of who we are as eternal beings. When we become born again, the Holy Spirit, metaphorically, buries Himself in that sand. The Holy Spirit embeds Himself in our human spirit.

We actually become a type of new species. We have the spirit of God now living in us. 2 Corinthians 5:17 says, *"Therefore, if anyone is in Christ, he is a new creation; old things have passed away; behold all things have become new."* We become a new spiritual force on the Earth. As children of God, we carry spiritual authority as sons and daughters of the Most-High God.

However, very few Christians throughout history have tapped into the spiritual authority that God has endued us with. It wasn't their fault. They operated in the knowledge they had. However, since the time of Martin Luther, our spiritual understanding has increased with each new generation and revelational knowledge has come into the church. We now stand on the shoulders of the healing revival preachers that brought the church a new understanding of God's will to heal and restore. We stand on the shoulders of the "Word of Faith" teachers that taught us the importance of faith and standing on the Word.

I do believe it is time for the church to step into a new revelation of who we are in Christ in a much greater capacity. We must learn how to recognize and purge wickedness within ourselves. And we need to develop our discernment to hear God more clearly. We must gain a much greater understanding of faith, authority, and responsibility as believers.

If we look around, there are several signposts that point to the conclusion that we are the generation that will usher in the return of Christ. 1 Peter 2:9 says, *"But you are a chosen generation, a royal priest-hood, a holy nation. His own special people, that you may proclaim the praises of Him who called you out of darkness into His marvelous light."* I do believe this scripture is talking about us. We are a chosen generation that will rise up and accomplish God's purposes on Earth.

We need to get a fresh revelation that God dwells within us. We are not mere men. We are a royal priesthood that was chosen for "such a time as this" to be in God's end-time army. Each of us has been hand-picked and equipped to carry out specific duties and assignments for God.

Our Subconscious Mind

What gets in the way of us being used by God to create positive change on Earth? Christians are in the habit of always blaming the devil because it is Satan's objective to rob, steal, and destroy. However, oftentimes, our failure to accomplish good isn't even the devil's fault. Surprisingly, it's the deficiencies in our soul that limit, hinder, and often stop us in our tracks.

Our subconscious mind is part of our soul and not part of our spirit. Our spirit is the home of the Holy Spirit, and that is the part of us that has been made brand new when we accepted Christ into our life. We know that our subconscious mind wasn't made completely new when we became a Christian. While some bondages and bad habits may have fallen away, most of us still have bad habits, wrong thoughts, insecurities, and self-sabotaging behaviors.

Usually when God talks to us, it isn't with a burning bush or an angelic visitation. Normally, the Holy Spirit speaks to us from our spirit. The problem is people haven't learned how to discern the voice of Holy Spirit. When the Holy Spirit speaks to us, His voice travels from our spirit and through our subconscious mind before it is registered in our conscious mind. Even spiritually mature people can have difficulty discerning the voice of the Holy Spirit in their lives. True, some haven't developed their discernment enough to pay attention and hear what God is telling them. But there are a lot of Christians that have flawed discernment because they have too much junk in their subconscious mind that blocks and distorts the subtle promptings of the Holy Spirit.

Our soul has two sections: our conscious mind and our subconscious mind. Our soul still has a carnal, Adamic nature that we need to *"renew to the word of God"* (in Christian terms, Romans 12:2) or clean up and educate (in worldly terms). We need to renew both our conscious mind and our subconscious mind.

While the Bible doesn't use the term subconscious mind, there is a verse in the Bible that defines it. Hebrews 4:12 reads, *"For the word of God is living and powerful, and sharper than a two-edged sword, piercing even the division between soul and spirit, and of joints and marrow, and is a discerner of the thoughts and intents of the heart."*

Before I teach on the conjunctions in this verse, I want to first comment on the first part of this scripture. It says the word of God is *"living and powerful."* When we read the Bible, new revelations and insights can spring forth. The Holy Spirit can highlight a scripture that we have read a hundred times. He can breathe new life on it and cause us to see it in a slightly different way. When Martin Luther read *"the just shall live by faith"* in the Bible, suddenly a metaphoric lightbulb turned on. He had a fresh revelation that people are saved by faith and not works. Even in the last hundred years, the church has gained insights and revelations that earlier Christians didn't have.

Certainly, everyone's experience can be a little different. But after I received the Baptism of the Holy Spirit with the evidence of speaking in tongues on August 8, 1994, the Bible came alive in a whole new way for me. Reading my Bible was noticeably different afterwards. It was like it went from a black and white movie to a fully colorized one. It wasn't just reading words on a page. There was life and vibrancy in every verse. There were nuances of insights with well-known verses and Bible stories.

Today, almost 30 years later, I wouldn't say that I still get fresh revelation out of every verse, passage, or chapter. But I would say that being a spirit-filled believer and receiving the Baptism of the Holy Spirit made it much easier to hear from God. Christians that have not experienced it may have a difficult time fully embracing the concept that the word of God is *"living and powerful."*

When we are synced up to the voice of the Holy Spirit, He will direct our steps. He will give us correction, direction, and affection through the scriptures. He may prompt us to read a verse a second time to draw our attention to it. Then, we may read a post on social media that touches on the subject. In another instance, we may over-hear a conversation in line at the grocery store, and we finally figure out that God is trying to get our attention about something. When we reread that verse God was trying to highlight to us, He may give us a new understanding of it, or He may give us guidance on how to handle a specific situation. The word of God is living and powerful and God uses the scriptures to lead and guide us every day.

This verse, Hebrews 12:4, is one of those verses that the Holy Spirit illuminated in a whole new way to me back in the mid-to-late 90's when God was teaching me about soul iniquities. As I was reading the verse one day, I sensed the Holy Spirit leading me to take each of the conjunctions and put them into two columns. When I did, a lightbulb flipped on in me. I believe the Holy Spirit illuminated to me that the first column references our conscious mind, and the second column refers to our subconscious mind.

The conjunctions I am referring to are the "and" phrases in the second half of the Hebrews 12:4 verse. They read, *"piercing even the division between (soul and spirit), and of (joints and marrow), and is a discerner of the (thoughts and intents) of the heart."*

Conscious Mind		Subconscious Mind
Soul	and	Spirit
Joints	and	Marrow
Thoughts	and	Intents

Let's look at the first column. The conscious mind is where we think and reason. The Bible's metaphor of a body part describes it as joint because the conscious mind is where thoughts are joined together. It is where we reason, where we plan, where we create. The conscious mind is where we connect information, form opinions, organize conclusions, and judge situations. We join together our education with our creativity and think up new ideas, procedures, and strategies. That first column tells us that our conscious mind is where our soul joins our thoughts together.

The second column describes our subconscious mind. To reiterate, psychology tells is that our beliefs and behaviors are driven from our subconscious mind. Our subconscious mind houses our true motives. The word *intent* is another word for motive. So, it appears that the Bible and psychology are in agreement that true motives are originated in the subconscious mind. We may reason and rationalize our beliefs and behaviors in our conscious mind, but our true motives and intents are housed in our subconscious mind.

What is marrow? Marrow is the dark, pasty substance inside our bones. It is hidden and not visible. I think it is so interesting that the Holy Spirit inspired the writer of Hebrews to use these two body parts (joints and marrow) to describe something that he didn't fully understand at the time.

Marrow is that part of the body where red blood cells are produced. The blood that is produced in the marrow is the life force of the entire body. What is made in the hidden part of the body is what brings oxygen and life to every organ, limb, and capillary in the body. Likewise, that which is produced in the most hidden place of our soul, our subconscious mind, is what drives our beliefs and behaviors and can be witnessed in our words, thoughts, and actions.

The marrow also is where our immunity is strengthened. Our immunity fights sickness and disease, and it is what keeps us healthy. Naturally speaking, when there is disease in the bone marrow, it makes the body weak, sick, and frail. When our immunity is compromised and weak, it shows outwardly, and our poor health is evident for others to see. Likewise, when there is sickness and disease in our subconscious mind, our behavior becomes ugly and evident for others to see.

And lastly, the marrow is where blood platelets are produced. Blood platelets assist in blood clotting, so we don't bleed to death when we are injured. I find this fascinating because our subconscious mind also has types of emotional blood platelets. We have emotional defense mechanisms like denial, repression, compartmentalization, and others that shield us emotionally when we can't handle the full emotional impact of a situation. They stop the emotional bleeding until we can process the psychological trauma in our life.

The Rudder

A rudder is what steers a ship. If the rudder is off course, the ship will never reach its desired destination. James 3:4 says, *"Look at the ship: although they are so large and are driven by fierce winds, they are turned by a very small rudder whatever the pilot desires."* Just as a small rudder steers a huge ship, so our tongues steer our lives.

Yes, we frame our life by the words of our mouth. However, the Bible also tells us that out of the heart the mouth speaks. Luke 6:45 says: *"A good man out of the good treasure of his heart brings forth good; and an evil man out of the evil treasures of his heart brings forth evil. For out of the abundance of the heart his mouth speaks."*

What are good treasures and evil treasures of a person's heart? They are the good and bad blueprints that reside in a person's subconscious mind. If a person is jealous, prideful, and spiteful, it will come out in their speech. Their "evil" or negative character qualities will shape their relationships, their life choices, and their success level. Likewise, when a person is kind, generous, and loving, they will sow those good qualities into relationships and will reap the same.

What is in Our Subconscious Mind?

The subconscious mind is one of the most misunderstood components of human beings. Two people can go through the exact same trauma in their life. One person regresses and wallows in the trauma, while the other is able to succeed and thrive in life. Of course, a person's personality temperament has a bearing on how emotional trauma affects them. However, what a person has residing in their subconscious mind determines how they react and function. The decisions that are made, the beliefs that are embraced, and the actions that are taken are all rooted in what a person has in their subconscious mind.

Our subconscious mind houses both good and bad elements:

- Our Faith
- Our Personality Temperament and Character Traits
- Our Comfort Zones, Limitations, Fears, and Insecurities
- Our Deep-rooted Emotional Wounds & Emotional Defense Mechanisms
- Our Diseases of the Soul
- Our Glitches

Most of these are self-explanatory. Some areas, I am just going to touch on briefly, while others I will go into a little more detail.

Our Faith

Surprisingly, most people really don't understand what faith is. I didn't until I started Bible school in 1994. And then, in that five-year period, between 1995 and 2000, when God was teaching me about the human soul, I grew to understand it in a greater way.

In its simplest definition, faith is believing, right? While it is true, it isn't true that what we believe in our mind is faith. There are really two kinds of believing. There is what we believe in our conscious mind, and there is what we believe in our subconscious mind. True faith is the latter. True faith is what we believe in our subconscious mind. When we read the word "heart" in the Bible, we would have a greater level of understanding if we substituted the word "heart" for "subconscious mind" as we read. Faith is what we believe in our heart (subconscious mind) not what we agree with in our mind.

Most Christians haven't caught the revelation that our subconscious mind can be a miracle factory. Mark 11:23 says, *"For assuredly, I say to you, whoever says to this mountain, 'Be removed and be cast into the sea' and does not doubt in his heart but believes that those things he says will come to pass, he will have whatever he says."*

Most people don't catch the revelation of this verse because they don't think the verse is true. Perhaps they have spoken to their mountain at different seasons in their life and didn't see any movement. So, while they appreciate the verse being in the Bible because it does offer them hope, most people don't really believe it is true. They haven't understood the *"does not doubt in his heart"* part. Most people have mental agreement with Bible promises, but that is very different than believing them in their heart (subconscious mind). Remember, the subconscious mind is like bone marrow. It isn't seen. Most people don't know exactly what does and doesn't reside in their subconscious mind. Their speech will offer clues but for the most part, it is hidden.

No other species on the planet has this amazing gift that God gave us. Think about it. God has given mankind the ability to create miracles. Mark 11:23 proves it. Jesus is telling us that mountains can actually move if we have faith for it in our heart. Christians have untapped power. Luke 24:49 talks about being *"endued with power when we receive the Holy Spirit."* Acts 1:8 says, *"But you shall receive power when the Holy Spirit has come upon you; and you shall be witnesses of Me in Jerusalem, and in all Judea and Samaria, and to the end of the Earth."* Is it any wonder why the devil has worked overtime to try to keep people ignorant and emotionally wounded? When our subconscious mind is wounded, weak, or diseased, we will often reject true faith so miracles can't develop.

Our Personality Temperament and Character Traits

The concept of personality temperament types has been around for thousands of years. There are different schools of thought on the subject. But one that has stood the test of time, came from the Greek physician Hippocrates. He developed four basic types into his medical theories (460-370 BCE). From then, and through modern times, they have been modified and used in many theories in medicine, psychology, and literature. 1) The Sanguine type is sociable, talkative, outgoing, and tends to be pleasure seeking. 2) The Choleric type is ambitious, logical, goal oriented, analytical, and tends to have a leadership drive. 3) The Melancholic type is self-reliant, thoughtful, extremely reserved, and is often artistic. 4) The Phlegmatic type is introverted, calm, unemotional, easygoing, patient, and agreeable.

Carl Jung was a Swiss psychiatrist and psychoanalyst and in 1921, he published a book entitled, "Psychological Types." He theorized that there are four psychological functions by which we experience life: sensation, intuition, feeling, and thinking.

Years later, a mother and daughter team (Katherine Cook Briggs and Isabel Briggs Myers) who had studied the Jung teachings extensively, turned his theory into psychological types for practical use. They developed a test to categorize people into 16 personality types. They worked on this during World War II, believing that knowledge of personality preferences would help women who were entering the industrial workforce at the time. This became known as the "Myer-Briggs Type Indicator (MBTI)."

In 1984, David Keirsey and Marilyn Bates, authored a book entitled, "Please Understand Me" where they examined each of the MBTI 16 personality temperament types. They detailed how each type of personality processed information, what strengths and weaknesses they usually had, how they tended to behave as a child, adult, parent, and co-worker. They authored a follow-up book in 2006 but I actually prefer the original one. I recommend this book for anyone who wants to understand human behavior. It details how we are all hard wired differently. Understanding these differences will make us more compassionate and forgiving towards those who don't think or feel exactly the way we do.

Our behavior is absolutely influenced by our personality temperament. However, there are no free passes for certain types of sins because those pet sins may be common for our personality type. We all have the power of choice. Every personality characteristic is like a coin. It can be used for positive or negative. It is up to us to flip the coin over and use our God-given personality traits for good and not for evil.

Our character is developed by our choices. If a child is allowed to get away with lying, it reinforces the behavior so that particular habit becomes a way of life. The same is true with any character issue. If areas are not confronted then they can become a stronghold in our life and once this occurs, they become second nature. A sin uncorrected will become a habit. A habit unconfronted will become our character.

Our Comfort Zones, Limitations, Fears, and Insecurities

For some people, the idea of change is terrifying, even if those changes are positive ones. Human nature, unfortunately, will desire and seek out what is familiar to us even though it is not good for us. Why do people stay in abusive relationships? Because what is known is more comfortable than choosing what is not known. The psychological pull of our comfort zones can, and often does, sabotage our success.

When we are used to struggling financially and sudden success starts to take us to a new financial level, our comfort zone will often cause us to sabotage opportunities. Self-sabotaging behavior can start to manifest through us. We may start showing up late to our job. Our performance may be substandard. Or we may get into unnecessary disputes. Without it even registering in our conscious mind, we could be messing up to keep us from succeeding and excelling on the job.

Recently, two friends of mine made huge mistakes in their life because they made decisions based on what they had done in the past. I tried to give them counsel before they made their decisions, but I was ignored, and they went with what felt comfortable for them.

People self-sabotage all the time because we obey the limitations in our subconscious mind that tells us how successful we can become. We sabotage business opportunities and relationships because of the subconscious walls and borders we have erected. In financial matters and business advancement, a person will usually start to unknowingly disrupt and impair their success, so it doesn't increase beyond what their comfort level can handle. In dating scenarios, it is common for both men and women to sabotage and limit their relationships because of their fear of emotional and even physical intimacy. Their comfort zone fears have caused many single people to walk away from relationships they should have embraced.

Our Deep-rooted Emotional Wounds & Emotional Defense Mechanisms

I think it is a fair assessment to say that most people have had emotional traumas and dramas in their past. Even if they were raised by near perfect parents, they still have experienced disappointments, tragedies, or betrayals. Some emotional wounds are processed months or years after the initial incident. While other people simply bury that wound in their heart and ignore the issue.

Psychology tells us that we have Emotional Defense Mechanisms. Just like blood platelets assist in blood clotting so we don't bleed to death physically, Emotional Defense Mechanisms can clot our emotional bleeding. When there is a potential for us to become emotionally over-whelmed, it is not uncommon for one of these mechanisms to activate within us on a subconscious level. These mechanisms may get initiated within us and we may not know it. Here are ten common ones:

Denial – Denial is one of the most common emotional defense mechanisms. A person in denial just simply blocks that issue in their mind. They don't think about it and can even act like the situation didn't happen. I know many women that have had an abortion that they have simply swept under the rug in their conscious mind. They haven't allowed themselves to think about it and process the gravity of their actions. People can also be in denial about health issues. Some-one very close to me had a large lump in her breast for years but refused to seek medical attention. She was in denial about it. Later, when the cancer had metastasized, she said she didn't mention it to her family or friends because she was standing in faith for her healing. She incorrectly labeled her denial as faith but there is a difference.

Repression – Repression is an interesting thing. Repression causes you to block a memory or situation because you aren't emotionally equipped to handle it. I do have experience with it. When I was 19 or 20 years old, I was walking to my car after my Psychology 101 class in college. The professor had been talking about memory repression. All the sudden, a memory of childhood molestation came back to my awareness while I was standing at the cross walk. I had been molested by someone who was 13 years older than me when I was in elementary school. I had forgotten all about it through my middle and high school years. Repressed memories are common for victims of molestation. I know men and women who didn't remember the abuse they ex-perienced until much later in life when they were more emotionally equipped to handle the memories.

Projection – Projection is misattributing thoughts, actions, and faults onto someone else. It is very common for a person to label others as having the same sins or weaknesses that they have. For example, if a person has jealousy, they may project that onto others and judge them for their perceived jealous behavior. Or if you don't care for someone, you may project and assume they don't like you.

Displacement – Displacement is also a common behavior. An example would be if you had a bad day and took it out on someone else. You may be mad at yourself or your boss, but rage against your family. You may snap at your child or your spouse because you have pent up anger and frustration. It never ceases to surprise me how people think they get a free pass to vent and act out on others when they have had a rough day. It is never okay to use your loved ones as a whipping post.

Regression – Regression can happen when a person is afraid or has anxiety which they try to escape by regressing to an earlier stage of life. In a child, that may mean they self sooth by sucking their thumb, or they want their childhood blanket. Their actions take them to their younger days that brought them comfort. In adults, regression may be overeating comfort foods, or curling up on the couch and watching mindless entertainment. When life seems too overwhelming, some people regress to activities that bring them comfort and peace.

Rationalization – Rationalization is so common it is difficult to even label it as an emotional defense mechanism. I believe everyone on the planet rationalizes their behavior to justify it and make sense of their negative thoughts and actions. It is human nature, and it is why everyone lives in their own version of reality. People believe their own rationalizations and fail to see that there is, most likely, an uglier motive in their subconscious mind that is driving that belief or behavior.

Sublimation – Sublimation is considered a positive technique for channeling frustration or anger. It happens when a person channels or redirects their aggression into an activity like boxing or other forms of exercise. This converts negative behaviors to constructive ones.

Reaction Formation – Reaction formation is a defense mechanism where people realize how they should be feeling but they act the exact opposite. They choose not to react, scream, cry, and pitch a fit when they are angry or frustration. Instead, they act overly positive and happy.

Compartmentalization – Compartmentalization is separating your life into different compartments. For example, when you leave the office, you don't give work a second thought until you head into work the following day. When someone lives a double life or has a secret sin, they will often compartmentalize that area of their life, so they don't feel guilty the rest of the time.

Intellectualization – Intellectualization is where you don't allow yourself to feel emotional about a situation because the emotions may be too overwhelming. I don't think this is such a bad thing. In fact, I think it can be a good idea when you need to hear from God concerning a situation. Several years ago, someone told me some terrible news. Before I reacted emotionally, I went to God and asked if it was true. God didn't give me an answer. I then asked God, "What should I do?" God said, "Stay the course, I will steady your hand." I believe not reacting in emotion actually helped me have clearer discernment on how to handle that situation. I have had other situations where I did react to a situation emotionally and my anger clouded my discernment. It was a lot harder to navigate the situation. Yes, we are emotional beings but not jumping to conclusions or allowing ourselves to dive headfirst into an emotional response can be a good thing. Before we react emotionally, ask God questions and listen for the answers first.

And finally, to finish out the list, our subconscious mind carries *Our Diseases of the Soul* and *Our Glitches.* I will go into detail over the next two chapters on these two components in our subconscious mind.

What Do You Believe?

To reiterate, we are a spirit, we have a soul, and we live in a body. Our soul is made up of both our conscious mind and subconscious mind. Our true motives/intents reside in our subconscious mind, whether we are consciously aware of our true motives or not. And our beliefs and behaviors are driven by our subconscious mind.

We can discover what we believe by our observing our behavior. James 2 tells us, *"Faith without works is dead."* What is faith? Faith is believing something in our heart/gut/subconscious mind. What we believe will be demonstrated in our works (our actions and behaviors). So, if our actions don't line up with what we think we believe, then we really don't believe it in our gut. For example, we may say we are trusting God for financial freedom, but if our words and actions are full of worry and fear, then we aren't really trusting God. We are not in faith; we are in hope. The same test can be done to see if we really have faith for healing. Fear and faith are opposites so if we are afraid than we aren't in faith. Real faith has a *know-that-I-know* element to it. Real faith has peace attached to it.

I want to challenge you, the reader, to examine what you believe. What promises of God are you standing in faith for? What promises are still in the "hope so" stage? What do you believe about yourself?

We cannot achieve success unless we believe we are successful. There is an old adage that says, "You are who you think you are, or you become it." That phrase is really just another way of saying, *"As a man thinks in his heart, so is he."* as it says in Proverbs 23:7. What we believe about ourselves will determine our success level.

If our subconscious identity believes we are fat, then we will stay fat no matter what pills we take or surgeries we have. Our bodies will self-sabotage to line up with the identity we believe about ourselves. If we have a poverty mentality, we will sabotage opportunities for success. If we believe we are unlovely, we will sabotage opportunities to find true love.

We can't fix a problem unless we know it exists. That is why it is necessary to take an inventory of ourselves and what we believe about ourselves. Are there negative identity-shaping words that were spoken to you as a child that you have embraced as part of your identity? Did someone call you "stupid" or "poor" or "a loser" and have you allowed any of those names to get branded onto your soul?

Renewing our mind to the Word of God isn't just about learning the Bible and uprooting iniquities. It's also about allowing God to infuse our subconscious mind with new, positive labels. Old identity-shaping words get replaced with new ones. Labels of "stupid, failure, ugly, and loser..." get replaced with "overcomer, victorious, apple of His eye, mind of Christ, and all-together lovely." God needs a people who will walk in confidence to be His ambassadors on Earth. If we don't allow God to fix our identity, then we won't walk in the confidence to carry out the assignments He has for us.

Fully Sanctified

We must renew both our conscious mind and our subconscious mind to the word of God. What does that mean? It means we need to *"take every thought captive"* as it says in 2 Corinthians 10:5. We need to pay attention to the thoughts that cross our mind and capture or arrest the wrong thoughts that shouldn't be allowed to be embraced. It means we have to be intentional about getting the word of God in our mind and heart. We need to meditate so the word of God not only fills our conscious mind, but that it sinks down into our subconscious mind and starts to change our identity.

If we don't renew our subconscious mind, we will continue to self-sabotage ourselves. The apostle Paul understood self-sabotage. He said in Romans 7:15, *"For what I am doing, I do not understand. For what I will to do, that I do not practice; but what I hate, that I do."*

For many of us, most of our blatant external sins fell away when we developed our relationship with God. However, our internal, subconscious iniquities don't just fall away. They need to be intentionally purged. We can't repent of something if we don't recognize the sin. Internal iniquities like pride, jealousy, and unforgiveness pop up in our life, but they get ignored for some reason.

1 Thessalonians 5:23 says, *"Now may the God peace Himself sanctify you completely; and may your whole spirit, soul and body be preserved blameless at the coming of the Lord Jesus Christ."* This verse is very insightful. Frist of all, it suggests that our "spirit, soul, and body" should be sanctified and renewed. The core of our human spirit where the Holy Spirit resides doesn't need sanctifying. That is why I believe when the Bible uses the word "spirit" in this verse, it is referring to our subconscious mind which does need sanctifying. The second thing I find interesting is the latter part of the verse. It says, *"be preserved blameless at the coming of the Lord Jesus Christ."* This suggests that when Jesus returns for the bride of Christ, we are finally going to have our act together and we will know how to uproot the ugly junk (our spots and wrinkles) from our subconscious mind.

I whole-heartedly believe it is the junk in our subconscious mind, it is our spots and wrinkles, that limits our discernment and limits the spiritual authority we walk in.

Matthew 5:8 says, *"Blessed are the pure in heart for they shall see God."* This verse has so many nuances of revelation.

One, people with a pure heart, or rather, people without a lot of negative stuff in their subconscious mind will be blessed. They will be blessed financially because their identity won't sabotage their success.

Two, they will be blessed financially because they won't have ugly motives and behaviors that turn customers and employers off. When people have deep-rooted iniquities, they cause clients and co-workers to shy away from them. Without really being able to put their finger on the exact cause, people with ugliness in their subconscious mind provoke others to pull away from them. Whereas people with a pure heart have much healthier and happier relationships. People want to do business with good people so success will follow them.

Three, some Christians that live in lack, think the closeness to God thing, the *"shall see God"* thing, excludes them from financial success and relationship success. They rehearse thoughts that God provides their needs but not their wants. They lean in on God being their best friend when people fail them. These thoughts promote the idea God doesn't want them blessed financially and that God doesn't want them to have close friends. If they don't believe it is God's will that they are financially blessed, they will sabotage financial opportunities. If they believe God alone is their close friend, then they won't work on their behavior around others to cultivate friendships. Jesus is preaching in Matthew 5 that we will be blessed if we have a pure heart. That sounds like it is God's will for us to be blessed.

Four, the verse reads, *"the pure in heart shall see God."* This implies that those with a pure heart will have better discernment. They will see and hear what God is telling them. When a person has diseased areas of their soul, it can block or distorted what the Holy Spirit tries to tell them.

Closing Thoughts

The human subconscious mind has been ignored and misunderstood for too long in the church. The subconscious mind is our miracle incubated. When Jesus told us we can curse a fig tree and it will die or we can speak to a mountain and command it to move, He was telling us the level of power that true faith has. Faith is not mental agreement with what God says. True faith is believing in our heart, our gut, our subconscious mind. It is time we understood this better so we can do the works that Jesus did, as the Bible says.

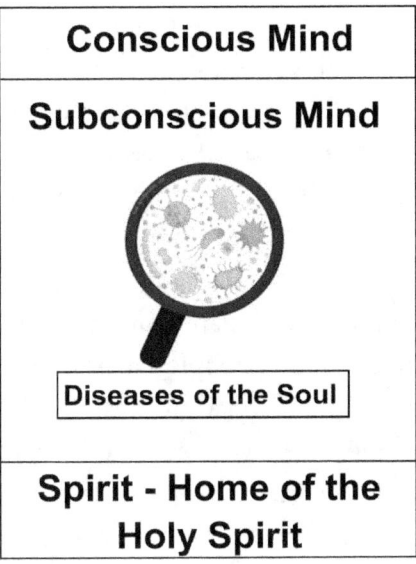

Conscious Mind

Subconscious Mind

Diseases of the Soul

Spirit - Home of the Holy Spirit

Three

Diseases of the Soul

I am sure that some of you are seeing the phrase *Diseases of the Soul* and you are wondering what the term means and where it came from. *Disease of the Soul* is the name of my first published book. That book was written in 2000 but I didn't attempt to get it published until 2003.

In the summer of 1995, I was at Christian conference at the Anaheim Convention Center, and I was sitting on a grassy knoll between the afternoon and evening meetings. A woman in her 30's approached me and started talking to me. She said God had just told her to share the phrase and concept of *Diseases of the Soul* with me. She said she knew God wasn't going to use her to teach it to the body of Christ but that she was just supposed to share the phrase and concept with someone else. She said she had originally thought she was supposed to give the phrase to Kenneth Hagin or Oral Roberts but God had just told her that I was the one that she was supposed to share it with. She said, "God is going to teach you about it and develop the concept and then you are supposed to teach it to the body of Christ." She demonstrated the concept by taking a piece of paper and making several small holes in the paper. She said, "When people have diseases of the soul, they miss revelation because the revelation falls on a diseased area." After she finished, she seemed to have a sense of completion like she had obeyed God and then she left.

I received that prophetic word, but I didn't attempt to manufacture a teaching on it. I simply went about my life and God used situations, people, and experiences to teach me a more comprehensive understanding of the topic over a five-year period.

God would teach me by doing stuff like waking me up in the middle of the night and telling me, "Compare *diseases of the soul* with the parable of the soil." He would highlight a person's behavior and say things like, "She is putting someone down to make herself look better. That is a manifestation of jealousy."

God directed my steps so I would be taught enough psychology to framework what He was showing me but not so much that it would override what He wanted me to understand spiritually. I believe God wanted me to focus on the spiritual side of subconscious sin, and not get too consumed with psychological explanations.

I had studied psychology in college, but God used an 80-hour real estate sales training I had in 1997 that brought a whole new level of understanding about the human conscious mind and subconscious mind. Some of the key take-aways from that 80-hour program were instrumental in God teaching me about *Diseases of the Soul.* In fact, some of the concepts from that course have been quoted in this book already.

They are:

- Ten percent of our brain is our conscious mind, and the other ninety percent is our subconscious mind.
- Our beliefs and behaviors are driven from our subconscious mind, not our conscious mind.
- People can be unaware of what resides in their subconscious mind.

What are Diseases of the Soul?

Simply put, *diseases of the soul* are propensities or bents towards certain types of sin. They are our weaknesses, our pet sins, our iniquities.

Most people think the word *iniquity* is just another name for sin. And while the two words can be synonymous, the word *iniquity* is also defined as the character of a sin. So according to that definition, *diseases of the soul* are *iniquities* because they are propensities toward a specific type or character of a sin.

When most people think of sin, they assume there is always a temptation and people make a choice to do wrong instead of doing what is right. However, with bents towards certain types of sin, a person can make a comment or take an action in almost an autopilot manner, and they may not realize that their comment or action was rooted in an iniquity residing in their subconscious mind. A large percentage of sins committed that are motivated by a person's soul iniquities are autopilot responses. They usually are not thoughtfully considered before the person chooses to take an action.

Here are the 12 *diseases of the soul* discussed in my 2003 book: 1) pride, 2) fear, 3) unforgiveness/offense, 4) jealousy/envy, 5) rebellion, 6) religious pride, 7) prejudice/hatred, 8) weak willpower, 9) sexual sins, addictions, and fetishes, 10) idolatry, 11) greed/selfish ambition, and 12) negative/critical/judgmental attitudes.

We don't view our pet sins as sins. When we make a comment or take an action that is rooted in our pride, we don't think it's wrong. We can justify our actions to ourselves and others, so it doesn't feel like a sin. Another example would be your co-worker friend said disparaging comments about another employee. Her comments were slanderous and vilified the other co-worker. Yet, in her mind, she didn't do anything wrong. She didn't recognize that her assassination of the co-worker's character was based out of jealous in her own heart. All of us, like that co-worker, can explain away and justify our pet sins and we refuse to see the damage they can cause.

Who has *Diseases of the Soul?*

If the average Christian looks at the list of the 12 *diseases of the soul,* they may pick out a couple of them that they think they have. However, a significant percentage of people have *diseases of the soul* that they are unaware of. There is a lady I have known for a couple of years and by my observation, she has at least eight of them. Her diseases feed off each other so, needless to say, she is not pleasant to be around. However, most people have between two and six soul iniquities by my estimation.

How do you know if you have a specific *disease of the soul?* Ask yourself some questions. Is it a stronghold? Are your beliefs or behaviors influenced by that soul disease? Do you manifest any of the common behaviors of someone with that iniquity? (The common behaviors for *diseases of the soul* will be discussed in Chapters 5 through 16).

In late spring of 1995, I was sitting in a Bible college class and the instructor said, "Ask God if there is anything stopping you from stepping into your destiny right now?" I asked the question, and I heard in my spirit, "Pride." My immediate reaction was to reject what the Holy Spirit had just told me. I thought, "No way! God, do you know what I have been through?" By that time in my life, it was a lot. I had been through significant loss and tragedy which brought me to my knees and back to God after being backslidden for almost ten years. I was fully committed to God and enrolled in a Bible school. I had gone through ten months of humbling myself and obedience to God. I didn't see any pride in my life.

After God told me I had pride, my life circumstances changed again. I suddenly found myself rejected by several people who I thought were my friends. I studied pride for about a year. I read the book of Jerimiah a few times as well as other segments of the Bible. I sincerely repented of pride even before I saw how it had manifested in my life. Slowly, God began to teach me about pride, and He showed me ways it was exhibited in my life.

God telling me I had pride was my first experience with a soul iniquity. And when the woman at the conference gave me the phrase *diseases of the soul* a few months later, I knew that pride was one of those soul diseases the woman was talking about.

Everyone has soul iniquities. For too long, we have excused our carnal propensities as just features of our personalities. But they aren't personality characteristics; they are pet sins.

They are Soul Cancers

I wrote my first book, *Diseases of the Soul* more than 20 years ago. At the time, the book's publisher didn't like the title of the book. They thought no one would read a book called *Diseases of the Soul* because it sounded too negative. And people have told me that through the years, as well. However, recently, as I was working on this book, I reflected on the term *diseases of the soul.* I felt like God told me that the ugliness of the term was intentional. God said, "People don't recognize how ugly their *pet sins* are. They need to see the ugliness so they will make an effort to uproot them." So yes, the term *diseases of the soul* does conjure up negative and even gross mental images.

We treat our *pet sins* as insignificant, but *diseases of the soul* are like cancers in our heart. They are growths, spots, areas of infection. Like a cancer, they can grow undetected within us for years. They can even metastasize and spread. And by the time we discover them, it can be too late. They could cause the death of important relationships. They can destroy careers. And they could cause the demise of our God-given promises and destinies.

How can *diseases of the soul* mutate and spread? Well, one example that comes to mind was in my brother Ken's life. He had a root of unforgiveness and offense towards our father that started at an early age. Yes, our father was controlling and, like many fathers in the 60's and 70's, his word was the final say. When Ken was in 6th or 7th grade, our father made him get a short haircut when the trend at that time was longer hair. So instead of Ken getting a John Denver haircut, he had to get a military style haircut. Ken was furious at our father and that incident forever solidified my brother's opinion of him. That root of unforgiveness grew and his disdain towards him was present his whole life. I believe that event, coupled with the knowledge that a *generational curse* of offense can run in my father's bloodline, was what embedded a stronghold of unforgiveness. So yes, Ken carried offense towards our father all his life. But he also had a *root of offense* that would cause him to get easily offended, and then hold onto that offense for years over seemingly insignificant events. That character trait of being easily offended and holding grudges stayed with him his whole life.

That root of unforgiveness towards our father spread to a soul cancer where almost everyone Ken knew had wronged him in some way and he harbored multiple grudges at any given time. He, of course, couldn't see and wouldn't acknowledge how he had hurt others. Yet, he was always the victim, and he would often plot revenge. I can't tell you the number of calls and texts I received from him venting about a hired mover that stole from us when the family estate was sold. He looked up the guy and left him several voicemails with threats. Ken didn't understand why I didn't have the same anger when the guy stole some of my sound equipment. Ken would call me up, years after the fact, just fuming and rehearsing the offense in his head.

Not only did Ken's initial root of unforgiveness/offense he had towards our father spread to other people, it spread to other *diseases of the soul* as well. Ken developed a root of rebellion which is a common occurrence when there is unforgiveness towards an authority figure. He became the ultimate non-conformist, which translated meant, he was flakey and undependable. He did things on his timetable and no one else's or he didn't do them at all.

Those two strongholds of offense and rebellion progressively manifested towards most authority figures. Teachers were tyrants. Bosses were only in it for the money and didn't care about their employees. Police officers were evil and on their own power trips. Ken's disdain for our father, the first authority figure in his life, grew to a dislike towards other authority figures, even God. Those strongholds affected how he perceived God for the majority of his life. Because Ken perceived his natural father as a dictator and mean-spirited, he started perceiving God that way too. I am happy to say Ken's resentment and hostility towards people and God lightened up dramatically towards the end of his life and he made peace with God before he passed away. But for the majority of his 58 years of life on Earth, he seethed hatred towards dozens of people. If things were on friendly terms with one of his enemies and something happens that Ken didn't approve of, he would quickly flip the switch and vilify that person again. His view of reality made his world dark and ugly, and most of it was all in his head.

Congenital Diseases

Not only do individuals have *diseases of the soul*, but entire churches can have them. It is not uncommon for most of the pastoral team, staff, volunteers, and congregation to have the same *disease of the soul* and be completely unaware of it. People with the same *disease of the soul* tend to gravitate towards each other. If you take a room full of complete strangers and keep them there for three hours, I guarantee you the people with a root of jealousy will find each other and form a friendship. The same is true in churches, so it makes sense that people would feel the most comfortable in a church that has the same issues.

A church in the deep south may carry prejudice and the manifestations are so subtle that they don't even notice. An outsider may visit the church and pick up on the subtlety of it but those that participate in it, don't see it. They may think the visitor is race baiting or being too sensitive if anything is said.

Another church can carry greed, where everything is about money. Yes, God wants His church and His people financially secure and prosperous. But there can be a wrong root developed and nurtured if every sermon is about money and everyone in the congregation is just pumped up with selfish ambition. Please don't misconstrue what I am saying. Most churches do not teach Biblical economics enough and most Christians have a poverty mentality. Most Christians need to renew their conscious mind and subconscious mind in the area of finance, so they stop sabotaging their success. However, there is a line that some churches cross without knowing it, and they have too much of their focus on money. Biblical economics is just one part of the gospel message, and it is wrong to ignore so many other relevant and needed subject matters in church.

Religious pride is also a common *disease of the soul* that is in a lot of churches. Some churches pride themselves in *"rightly dividing the word of truth"* as the Bible says in 2 Timothy 2:15. They embrace a self-righteous posture and look down on other pastors and churches from their perch of perceived of superiority. They believe their version of truth is the ultimate truth and they scoff at other churches.

There are also churches with a stronghold of unforgiveness. Most church members in those churches seem to carry emotional wounds and many of them embrace a *victim mentality.* Most sermons coddle emotional wounds and justify the people's right to hold on to offenses – all under the label of promoting emotional healing. The pastors agree with the offense and make the people feel vindicated in their position of unforgiveness.

Churches can act like *patient zero and* can cause the development or growth of a specific *disease of the soul* within a member of the congregation. However, even with that risk, it is better to attend church than to not attend a church. The Bible says in Hebrews 10:25, *"don't forsake the assembling of the saints."* When Christians are isolated, they don't have the covering and spiritual protection of the local church. Isolation can also lead to depression and/or goofy thinking.

What Causes Diseases of the Soul?

Diseases of the soul can either get stronger and more ingrained or slowly uprooted by our daily choices. Our conscious mind is the gateway to our subconscious mind. The battlefield really is in the mind. When we don't *"take every thought captive"* (as it says in 1 Cor. 10:5) and chaperon our thoughts, we open the door to all kinds of strongholds in our life. When we don't treat a wound when it's just an infection and deal with it while it is still visible, we invite that issue to sink its roots down into our soul. Our infections can turn into diseases if we allow them. And once a disease takes root and goes underground, it can be harder to see.

Diseases of the soul can come in all shapes and sizes. Some people can have enormous iniquity strongholds that they have fed for years. While others can have small, weak ones that haven't been allowed to grow very strong.

The core, or nucleus, of a *disease of the soul* is one of three things: 1) a generational curse, 2) a past wound or traumatic event, or 3) a demonic stronghold. Or, it can be a combination of any of these three root causes.

A Generational Curse

I am sure there are those that don't understand or agree with the concept of *generational curses.* Truly, I understand why people would reject the concept. However, I can't disagree with the theory for two reasons. 1) I have experienced it first-hand. And 2) It's in the Bible.

In my own family, my father had a root of unforgiveness and to listen to his stories about his father, it was easy to see my grandfather had it too. And my brother Ken certainly had it. But that particular iniquity didn't show up in all my father's biological children. I don't know why it would affect one child and not another. Could a child's personality temperament be a factor?

I do believe a person can take measures to ensure they don't embrace the same iniquities as their parents. An ex-boyfriend had a father that was an alcoholic. And even though my boyfriend had that addictive pull, his hatred for drunkenness kept him far away from that vice.

The concept of generational curses is in the Bible. Exodus 34:6-7 says, *"And the Lord passed before him and proclaimed, 'The Lord, the Lord God, merciful and gracious, longsuffering, and abounding in goodness and truth, keeping mercy for thousands, forgiving iniquity and transgressions and sin, by no means clearing the guilty, visiting the iniquity of the father upon the children and the children's children to the third and fourth generation.'"*

These two verses almost sound contradictory. It talks about God being merciful and forgiving and then it implies our iniquities will be passed on if they aren't cleared. Certainly, a quick little "forgive me" prayer doesn't uproot a stronghold embedded in a person's sub-conscious mind. Most of us know that uprooting something out of our subconscious mind isn't that easy. Perhaps these verses are suggesting that if a person is aware of their weaknesses and they repent from their soul strongholds, then those strongholds won't turn into *generational curses*. Exodus 34:7 says, *"...by no means clearing the guilty..."* – well, we know that true repentance absolutely clears the guilty. So, awareness of the iniquity and a repentant heart may stop our iniquities from being passed down as generational curses.

A Past Emotional Wound or Traumatic Event

Events from our past can absolutely cause *diseases of the soul*. When my mother was a child, she nearly drowned. I believe that traumatic event in her childhood was the cause of a stronghold of fear. She never talked about it although everyone in the family knew about her fear of water. She took showers, never baths. She would never go in a pool or the ocean. On houseboat family vacations, she always had her lifejacket on even when she was on shore.

In the 90's, when my parents were in their early retirement years, my father decided to have a pool installed so he could swim laps for exercise. Of course, my mother greatly opposed the idea. However, after lengthy discussions, she finally gave her consent when my dad said the pool wouldn't have a deep end. My father had a pool installed that had steps at both ends and the deepest part of the pool was three and a half feet deep. My father could swim his laps and if my mother fell in, she could just stand up.

Well, my mother did fall in their pool in the 2000's, and she almost drown again. She was skimming leaves out of the pool, lost her footing, and fell in. She was so emotionally traumatized by the fall that she forgot to just stand up. She thrashed in the water for a long time before she was able to get herself vertical. She failed to calm herself; as a result, she almost did drown.

My mother was a good, godly woman, but most of her thoughts, deliberations, and decisions all had fear as a motivating factor. In the years when my father was emotionally abusive and occasionally physically abusive, she obeyed her fear and didn't take actions to remove herself. True, there were very few social programs back then for woman who wanted to separate from their husbands. Fear of not having food, shelter, and a good reputation for her children forced her to endure emotional abuse.

The root of fear in my mother stole her peace and diminished her quality of life. She spent too much time worrying about everything.

Raising seven children is enough to cause any parent to worry, but my mother was obsessive with her worrying. What she considered prayer was often just mentally circling and rehearsing her concerns.

Two of the most common *diseases of the soul* that are formed from traumatic past events are fear and unforgiveness; I believe a high percentage of people carry both of these. For many, the scars of physical, emotional, or sexual abuse have left an indelible mark on human souls.

Everyone has past traumas and dramas. It is just part of living a human existence. Some people have lived through unimaginable circumstances. While others have emotional scars from situations that some may consider to be relatively mild. Everyone processes events differently. So, what may be insignificant to one person, may be devastating to someone else. Case in point, for most 12-year-old boys, being forced to get a haircut they don't like wouldn't even be a memory six months later. But for my brother Ken, it was a defining moment when seeds of disdain and unforgiveness towards our father took root. That offense linked arms with the *generational curse* of offense that was in his DNA, and it created a stronghold of unforgiveness and offense in my brother's subconscious mind.

Emotional wounds can be created by almost anything. A comment, a gesture, or any perceived wrong can become twisted and an offense can be created. Remember, it isn't always the wrongs that people have endured that have caused emotional wounds. It's oftentimes the perceived wrongs that have been concocted and embellished in a person's mind that has caused the emotional wound. A person can take a minor infraction or a misunderstanding and turn a speed bump into Mount Everest.

Demonic Oppression

Some Christian denominations (Presbyterian, Baptist, Methodist, Lutherans, and some Evangelical churches) do not believe Christians can have demons residing in them. They also tend to embrace the stance that some of the teachings and practices of Jesus and the first century Christians no longer apply to the church today like: the laying on of hands for healing, speaking in tongues, prophesying, and deliverance (casting out demons). Whereas most Spirit-filled denominations like Assemblies of God, Four Square, Church of God, Calvary Chapel, Vineyard, and Pentecostal churches do acknowledge the activities of demons and the practices of the first century church. But the degree of the belief and the amount they are practiced can vary quite a bit between the denominations and even individual churches. Most Spirit-filled churches believe the instructions Jesus gave His disciples also apply to us. Jesus said in The Great Commission in Mark 16:17-18, *"These signs will follow those who believe: In My name they will cast out demons; they will speak with new tongues; they will take up serpents; and if they drink anything deadly, it will by no means hurt them; they will lay hands on the sick, and they will recover."* (While there are some people who literally handle snakes, most spirit-filled believers do not condone the practice. An instructor at the second Bible school I attended went into a lengthy dissertation on why the literal translation of "will take up serpents" should really be translated "will drive away serpents.") Anyway, it was Jesus' instruction to His followers to cast out demons, pray in tongues, and pray healing over those who are sick.

I grew up in an evangelical church that dismissed healing, tongues, and deliverance. We were taught that spirit-filled, charismatic Christians were emotional, weird, and scripturally unbalanced. Demons weren't discussed except to say that a Christian can't have one. I was shocked when I came back to God, after being backslidden for almost ten years, to learn how much the New Testament talked about tongues, healing, and demons.

The debate of whether a Christian can have a demon or not was never a debate for me. Throughout my life, everyone in my family was a Christian, yet I witnessed demons manifesting through my father and my brother on several occasions. They both had anger demons. When they would get mad and they allowed that rage to manifest, their eyes would glaze over, and their demons would express themselves.

Both Bible schools I attended taught that a Christian can be oppressed by a demon but not be possessed by one. A Christian can have a demon in their soul and but not in their spirit where the Holy Spirit resides. The Bible colleges taught that possession is where a demon has taken residence in a person's spirit and that demon can manifest anytime it wants without the permission of the host human. Oppression is where a demon either hovers around a person externally or it has attached itself to a person's soul with their agreement. When a person is oppressed by a demon, the person still has control of their own actions. They have the authority to choose to allow that demon to manifest through them or to shut it down.

The problem is most people that have demons don't know they have them. They think all the random thoughts and emotions that are generated by the demon are really their own thoughts. As previously stated, demons like to hide. If they can camouflage as a person's personality quirks, they will.

The spirit world operates by agreement. Angels are activated when we agree with the word of God and speak it out. Likewise, demons are allowed access when we agree with demonic suggestions. When someone is depressed and all they do is meditate on and agree with negative thoughts, that can invite a depression demon into their life. Does everyone that is depressed have a demon in their soul? No, however, that dark cloud hanging over a person's head may not just be a metaphorical one.

When someone is buffeted with discouraging thoughts on a consistent basis, they may not have a demon in them, but certainly there is a demon tormenting their mind. I do not know the percentage of Christians that have demons in them verses there being an external demon that makes demonic suggestions. But I think it is fair to say that just like God assigns angels to us, the kingdom of darkness assigns demons to us. Those demons are probably going to attempt to tempt, discourage, and provoke us to anger if they can. When we have negative thoughts about ourselves or others and we think it is just our own self-talk, it can be demonic suggestions masquerading as our own thoughts.

So which *diseases of the soul* are more likely to have a demon at their core? There really isn't a clear-cut answer to that question. It depends on the person and how large of a stronghold that soul iniquity is. If someone is a pedophile, I believe they have a demon in them. As well, jealousy is sometimes called the "green-eyed monster." Certainly, not everyone with the soul disease of jealousy has a jealousy demon. However, if the person has allowed that sin to go unchecked and unfettered long enough where it has become a huge diseased area of their soul, there can absolutely be a demon at the core.

How Do We Identify Diseases of the Soul?

As I mentioned previously, a person may already know some of their *diseases of the soul* or there can be some iniquities that are blind spots to them. I was completely shocked when God told me I had pride. Even after the Holy Spirit told me I had it, I wanted to argue the point because I just didn't see it.

One way to identify any soul iniquities you may have is to simply ask God about them. You can go through the list of them and sincerely ask God about each one of them. However, don't be surprised if your internal knee-jerk answer will say "no" when the true answer from the Holy Spirit may be "yes." If and when you ask God about specific soul iniquities, try to make sure it is the voice of the Holy Spirit if you hear a "no."

God wants us to recognize our *diseases of the soul* because they can cloud our discernment and stop us from stepping into the assignments He has for us. But there are some people that will embrace the emotional defense mechanism of denial when confronted with their soul iniquities. Those people may need more teaching and revelation knowledge of God's love for them before they are ready to hear about their soul iniquities.

When some people acknowledge the ugliness of their sin, they may have a hard time reconciling their worth to God. They may start to view themselves as unlovely and therefore unlovable by God. Having an understanding of God's unconditional love and understanding that our righteousness is not in our own works but rather in the work of Calvary, will help people not react in denial. Christians that come from a Catholic background or from Arminian leaning churches may place too much emphasis on works and good deeds. As a result, they may measure their value to God only based on their performance and not the fact that we are made righteous through Jesus. Identifying their soul iniquities may be more difficult for them.

In addition to asking God which *diseases of the soul* you may carry, reading this book will help answer those questions as well. By reading the common manifestations for the soul iniquities, you may recognize those behaviors in yourself.

God's Timing

As you read this book, you will probably see some manifestations of soul iniquities that your friends and family possess. I caution you to ask God for wisdom before telling your friends or family what soul iniquities you think they have. You can lose friendships if you point out a person's flaws outside of God's direction. Most revelations about soul iniquities need to be done in God's timing.

A few months ago, I received an email from a female reader that had a copy of my book *Diseases of the Soul*. She said the book sat on her bookshelf for several years before she read it. She commented that she wished she knew the information in the book years before because it would have brought understanding that she was lacking. But she also understood why she sensed God leading her to read it when she did. She said God used the book to highlight some recent situations in her life to show her layers of truth. She said if she would have read the book when she first got it, she may have missed those nuances of revelation from her recent situations that God was trying to show her.

I had attended a Bible School in 1994 and 1995 but I also attended another Bible College from 1997 to 1999. While I attended the latter, I had a roommate, Maria, that I used to occasionally carpool with to church. During the drive, she made a comment that surprised me. When I got home, I asked God about it and His response was, "Jealousy." I couldn't see it in her. Maria had so many wonderful character qualities. She was kind, sweet, and giving. She was strong in the gifts of mercy and hospitality and was exceptional in the area of one-on-one evangelism. But then God said, "Look at her sisters, her siblings." Then, I began to see it. She had previously mentioned strife and contention among her sisters. God showed me that since we were close and we were like sisters in many ways, some sibling rivalry was being projected towards me.

When God told me Maria had jealousy issues, I decided it was just for my knowledge. I felt that I wasn't necessarily supposed to tell her. I struggled over the issue because I knew that only the Holy Spirit can open a person's eyes to see their own iniquity.

Then God set me up. A few days later, Maria started talking about jealousy among her sisters. She went on to say that the issue of jealousy had already been resolved and it wasn't an issue for her anymore. At that point, God told me to tell her what the Holy Spirit had told me a few days earlier. I obeyed and encouraged her to reexamine that area.

She reacted rather indifferently. Maria didn't outwardly accept or reject the information. Afterall, it didn't *bear witness* with her because it was a blind spot for her.

As time went by, I began to notice some inconsistencies in her personality. She would be very sweet, then unexpectedly she would project hostility towards me. A majority of the time, her actions were very subtle, and I suspect she was not even aware of them. If Maria was aware of her hostile behavior or if I mentioned it to her, she would provide some sort of reasoning to justify it. If the hostility was in the form of a criticism in front of other people, Maria's rationalization for her behavior was to make sure I didn't think more highly of myself than I ought. In her mind, there was always a logical reason for her behavior, and she wasn't aware that it stemmed from a subconscious root of jealousy. Maria's character attacks on me were thwarted because I knew it wasn't about me. She seemed to think we were in a competition, and we weren't.

I soon noticed that Maria was manifesting jealousy towards other people, not just me. She formed hostility towards some of the church leaders and other Bible College students. She was easily bugged by their comments or gestures. She would often try to spiritualize her negative attitudes towards them. Maria would label them as carnal if they got attention or received recognition for something. If students or leaders said something humorous, they were being carnal. If a preacher told too many personal stories, he was being carnal (So, in addition to jealousy, she suffered from religious pride.) Because Maria continually compared herself to others, she resented them when she saw traits in them that she didn't have, or she thought she didn't have. She then became disappointed in herself at her perceived weaknesses.

About a year after God had revealed that she had jealousy issues, it all came to a head. The hostility towards me had been dormant for a few months, then it resurfaced. One evening, we were at a bible school banquet, and Maria made a comment to discredit me in front of more than a dozen people.

I was hesitant to bring up her comment to her because I knew Maria wasn't consciously aware of her motive. I asked God if I was supposed to mention it. He asked if I was angry. I said, "No. I am perfectly happy with never mentioning it." A bit of time passed, and I sensed God telling me He did want me to address the comment to Maria. I spoke to her about it and told her that a couple of other people had approached me about it as well. Maria immediately got defensive, and the conversation didn't last long.

A short time later, Maria wanted to talk. She was visibly shaken. God had opened her eyes. As she talked, she started to recount how jealousy had manifested throughout her life and how it sabotaged aspects of her marriage and other relationships. Maria said she spent a good part of that night and the next day in tears of repentance before God. She said God revealed to her that it was a *generational curse* in her family tree and that it was a black spot in her soul. The next day, she mentioned how ugly and dirty she felt after seeing it.

When a *disease of the soul* is a blind spot to a person, the revelation of that soul spot needs to be in God's timing. Otherwise, it will be like my roommate's initial denial mentioned in the story above. They just won't see it until their heart is ready; and God arranges circumstances to show them their heart.

Closing Thoughts

When it comes to purging and uprooting iniquities out of our own hearts, I would normally advise to let God do it in His timing. However, there has been a shift in the timetable. I do not believe we have the luxury of procrastinating the purging of our iniquities any longer. With the current events happening on Earth today, it is clear to see that our time is short. God needs all Christians to get rid of their *spots and wrinkles* and to step into our purpose and activate the assignments He has for us. It is time for the church to uproot her soul iniquities, so we can have better discernment and walk in a greater authority.

Four

Our Glitches

A glitch is a mistake or irregularity. Do you remember in the first Matrix movie when Neo saw a black cat walk by the doorway, then he saw that exact same thing happen again? He was told that was a *glitch in the matrix* and to beware when that happens. In the movie, when someone experiences a *déjà vu* happening, it was a mistake in the Matrix A.I. system.

In the context of this book, a glitch is a repeating behavior. For those of us that are old enough to remember vinyl records, when there is a scratch in the record, it causes the same line to repeat over and over. And believe or not, most of us have autopilot type behaviors that we repeat even though those behaviors are either sinful or self-sabotaging. These glitches (scratches, lines, folds, wrinkles) in our subconscious mind can get triggered when we encounter a situation, emotion, or feeling that we have had in the past. As a result, we just repeat the belief or behavior in almost an autopilot manner.

If we consider the components of a computer, we can get a better understanding of the human psyche. Our spirit, the core of our being where the Holy Spirit resides, is like the motherboard. Our subconscious mind is like the hard drive that stores all our information and contains all our programing. Our conscious mind is like the monitor where we are able to see some of what has been loaded on the computer. We can see stored pictures and documents; allowing us to access and use programs that are on the hard drive. Our conscious mind only allows us to see some of what has been stored and programmed in our subconscious mind, much like the monitor only allows the user to see some of what is on the hard drive.

A monitor can be used to search the internet to see external information that is not on the hard drive. We can see information, pictures, stories, theories, ideas that we understand and agree with in our conscious mind, but that doesn't mean that information has been downloaded into our subconscious belief system. That is the error that most people make. We assume the sermons we hear and agree with are downloaded onto our hard drive, our subconscious mind, and they aren't. We can believe and totally agree with something in our conscious mind but that doesn't mean that the information has been downloaded or deposited into our subconscious mind where true faith and belief resides.

And finally, the keyboard represents programming. Words, symbols, numbers, and functions are used to write programming codes that modify what is on the hard drive and what is visible on the monitor. Computer programming is changed by what is typed. Our subconscious mind programming is changed by words we hear, say, see, and think about. Hebrews 10:17 says, *"Faith comes by hearing and hearing by the word of God."*

What is faith? Faith is believing something in our subconscious mind, our gut, whether that belief is something good or it is negative. Hearing the word of God can actually program faith into our subconscious mind. As well, hearing negative words can program our subconscious mind in a harmful way.

Why would someone believe they are stupid? They believe it because that is what someone called them when they were a child. Or they may believe it if they labeled themself that when they failed at something. That identity-shaping word became incorporated into their subconscious programming. Likewise, a Rhema word from God can be an identity-changing word that modifies the programming in a person's subconscious mind.

Just like we can have a virus on a hard drive that affects the performance of a computer, we can have viruses and glitches in our subconscious mind. *Diseases of the soul* are like computer viruses. They are diseased spots in our subconscious mind that can get triggered in certain situations. And negative beliefs and behaviors that repeat in an almost autopilot manner are like glitches on a computer's hard drive.

Autopilot Responses

In the last chapter, when describing *diseases of the soul*, I mentioned that they are iniquities that can be autopilot sinful responses where a person often doesn't deliberate a sinful temptation. Most of the time, people sin or self-sabotage without thinking about their behavior. Our glitches do exactly the same thing. Our glitches are autopilot repeating responses embedded into our subconscious mind.

Neuroscience tells us that streams of beliefs and patterns of behavior are established pathways in our mind. There are so many pathways that it only makes sense that we have ones that are not beneficial for us. But thank God, neuroscience also tells us we can *train our brain* and replace negative pathways with new positive ones. The biggest problem is most of our negative beliefs and behaviors go unchecked and unchallenged. They are rarely diagnosed. And they are usually not understood, so they are not dealt with properly.

A neuroscience instructor who was conducting a training that I attended, called our patterns of behavior *pathways in the brain,* but in my mind, I envisioned them like a complex freeway system. The last time I was in Dallas, I was completely amazed by the complexity of all of the highways, byways, overpasses, and offramps in the downtown Dallas area. It was a mess. Even with my navigational app on my phone, I still took wrong exits and ended up on streets I didn't want to be on. I immediately drew a parallel between the Dallas freeway system and the neuroscientist's pathways in the brain. If we think of our patterns of thoughts and behaviors like a giant roadway complex, we can understand how we can keep taking the wrong offramps of negative conclusions and behaviors.

In certain situations, we don't pay attention. Our mind is on other things as we take the roads (pathways) we are familiar with. We have all driven with our minds on other things and we have missed the offramp we had intended to take. Or, we have driven home on autopilot and forgot that we had planned on running an errand before going home. We weren't thinking about our driving as we were driving. Our mind was on something else. Yet, our internal autopilot kicked in as we thought about something that happened at work. The same is true for our thought patterns and negative behaviors. We take the offramps we are used to, even if it means we end up at destinations that weren't intended. They are our *normal*. And we are often blind to the fact that we need to establish a new *normal*.

How Did We Get Glitches?

Our glitches, our *broken record* behavior patterns, can have different root causes. The behavior can be: 1) A manifestation or trait from a *disease of the soul* that we carry. 2) A knee-jerk, autopilot response from our identity comfort zone. 3) An uncorrected behavior from our past.

1) Manifestation or Trait of a *Disease of the Soul*

Most of the *diseases of the soul* have common behavior manifestations, and those manifestations can be helpful in diagnosing which soul diseases a person carries. All of the common manifestations for a specific *disease of the soul* don't have to be witnessed in a person's behavior to detect if that person carries that specific soul iniquity. But we will typically see at least one or two of the common ones if a person has that specific soul iniquity.

A common expression of pride is lying. Lying can also be a demonstration of other *diseases of the soul*, however, it is the most common one for pride. Our pride tries to hide our weaknesses and sins, so we lie to cover up what we don't want others to know.

When researching for my book *Lopsided Relationships* (published 2019), I discovered that the average person lies 100 times a day. That is a huge number. Most of the lies are *little white lies* of exaggeration or omission of information.

Another example would be getting your feelings hurt if you have a root of unforgiveness. People with the soul iniquity of unforgiveness are extremely sensitive and their autopilot response is to feel attacked and wounded when somebody says or does something that hits a nerve. Yes, there are people that can take offense after they have had the chance to think about what was said or done but I'm not referring to that type of methodical deliberation. I am talking about people who have an auto-response, a glitch, of emotional pain when something triggers it. The offensive comment or action may not have even been noticed by anyone else in the room, but to the one with unforgiveness, it may have felt like a bullet to the heart.

Glitches, that are manifestations of a soul iniquity, can either be sins (like the lying) or they can be self-sabotaging (like getting your feelings hurt too easily). Either way, they are trigger responses of emotions or actions that demonstrate what is in our heart.

2) Our Identity Comfort Zone

Comfort zones were discussed in Chapter 2. But this section discusses how our comfort zones are often tied into our identity and cause auto-response emotional reactions and repeating behaviors.

If we are used to being financially broke, we will impair and disrupt opportunities for additional income. If we are used to being single, we will damage opportunities for a romantic relationship. If we are used to being fat, we will sabotage our weight loss goals. Our identity comfort zones control us more than we ever imagined.

Our subconscious comfort zones can also masquerade as our discernment. Case in point, I know a Christian woman who is single, and I believe her true heart's desire is to be married. However, when I have encouraged her to meet single Christian men her age, she always makes an excuse. When I have offered to create a profile for her on an online Christian dating app, she has rejected my offers. She tries to spiritualize her refusal by saying she "just doesn't have peace about it." We know God can use peace as an umpire as the Bible suggests in Colossians 3:15. Peace is an instrumental tool God uses to give us direction in our life. But my friend, like many Christians, mistakes fear of change and actions that are outside of her comfort zone, as a lack of peace and godly direction for her life. Just because something feels uncomfortable, doesn't mean it's not God's direction for our life.

"I Need Money"

The *"I need money"* glitch is one that was discussed in my book *Lopsided Relationships* in the chapter entitled *Money Moochers*. The subconscious command or voice in a person's head that tells them that they need money is a neurological pathway that has become part of that person's identity. The *"I need money"* subconscious blueprint expresses itself as a *poverty mentality* and the person either hoards money or they waste money.

The hoarder is someone who is extremely frugal regardless of how much money they have. Their fear of being broke causes them to frequently refrain from spending money on themselves or others.

Years ago, one of my mother's caregivers that had also rented a room from us was very frugal. She didn't hoard possessions. In fact, she was a minimalist. Normally, the trait of being careful with money would be a very admirable trait. However, the woman had sold her condo and had over $100,000 in the bank and she still pinched pennies like she didn't have a dime to her name.

One time, there was five of us going out to lunch after a group activity. It had been established by someone that we would all go *Dutch*. When it came time to order, my frugal caregiver/tenant/friend just ordered a scoop of vanilla ice cream for lunch. I knew she must have been hungry because she hadn't eaten anything earlier. I asked her privately why she only ordered a scoop of ice cream. She said because it costs $1.99, and it was the cheapest thing on the menu. I spent a couple minutes trying to convince her to change her order to the $6.99 lunch special because it was a lot of food for a good price. She had over $100,000 in the bank but she wouldn't reconsider her lunch order. I almost offered to pay for her lunch, but I stopped myself. She was the one who had to live with her decision and, quite frankly, her penny-pinching choices shouldn't be rewarded with a free lunch.

While the other women at the table were in another conversation, I asked her privately what she typically ordered at restaurants. She said she rarely ate at restaurants because it was cheaper to eat at home. I asked her what beverage she usually ordered when she did eat out. She said she always orders water since it is free.

After losing contact with each other, our paths crossed again seven or eight years later. We have chatted several times since then, and I am glad to say that several of her quirks, including her penny-pinching mindset, has diminished quite a bit.

The *"I need money"* subconscious glitch was well established within my brother Ken, as well. Except with him, it was the opposite from my mother's caregiver. His *"I need money"* subconscious command made him spend, waste, and give away any money he got. His *poverty mentality* was so entrenched into his identity that it was a neurological 8-lane freeway. It wasn't just a small dirt road he occasionally ventured down. For him, his identity kept replaying the broken record "I need money" so he subconsciously aligned his circumstances to line up with that command. There is an old adage, *"You are what you think you are, or you become it."* He always believed he needed money, so as he kept mismanaging it, his realty matched what he believed in his subconscious mind.

For as long as I can remember, Ken always had money issues. Even back in the 90's, he would continually ask to borrow money from me. If I were to estimate the total amount he borrowed from me, I would guess that it was over $50,000 over his lifetime and it was never paid back. There were three times when the balance was over $10,000, and I wiped the debt off and started a fresh tally.

He was irresponsible when it came to money management. If he borrowed money for his truck registration, I would have to literally give it to him when he was on his way to DMV. Otherwise, he would spend it, waste it, or give it away before he went to DMV. He had a habit of rationalizing his money issues. All new expenses would be an emergency and he always told himself he could spend what he had borrowed and the money he would get the following week could cover the cost of whatever he borrowed money for.

He lived with me for seven years in the 2010's when I was the trustee for the family estate after our father passed away. The money he made as an electrician and handyman was mostly given to his female friends in the Philippines. He used to come to me almost daily and ask for $2 to $20 dollars for different items. And no, he didn't pay for food, rent, or utilities in that seven-year period. He was broke all the time. That was his identity. That was his comfort zone even though you would think it would be extremely uncomfortable. It was what he was used to; it was his normal.

When he got big chunks of money, he quickly squandered it. In 2001, he received $10,000 as a portion of our sister Stephanie's life insurance and it was spent within a week. When he received an inheritance amount of $80,000 in 2017, he had spent it in about two and a half months. He bought a cheap truck ($2,800) and a motorcycle ($1,300). He lived in a Motel 6 for a couple of months, then he sent the rest of it to his friends in the Philippines.

I have known other people with the same money management challenges that stem from a subconscious *"I need money"* internal command, but Ken's was so dramatic, it was a good example. When people have this, they usually don't recognize it for what it is. They usually will have reasons and excuses for all their financial decisions. But when an issue isn't recognized then the record player just keeps playing. That scratch on their record causes the same lyrics (behaviors) to just keeps repeating.

The Fat Glitch

What we believe about ourselves can absolutely determine our glitches. Just like the *"I need money"* belief attached itself to my brother Ken's identity, our body image beliefs attach themselves to us and create glitches. What we believe about ourselves is our subconscious identity. If you think you are fat, you will become fat even if you weren't fat when the belief was embraced.

Why do 95% of the people that lose a considerable amount of weight gain it back within two years? In their conscious mind they want to be thin, but their subconscious mind houses their identity glitches that fight against the progress they have made. Most people end up sabotaging their weight loss success because they don't work on changing their identity comfort zones in the subconscious mind.

Imagine yourself thin. Speak identity shaping words over yourself. Ask God to give you dreams where you are thinner. Otherwise, as soon as you lose a few pounds, that repeating sabotaging behavior can resurface and reverse the progress you have made.

It goes back to Paul writings in Romans 7:15-19. Verse 19 is very similar to verse 15 (that was referenced earlier in the book.) Romans 7:19 says, *"For the good that I will to do, I do not do; but the evil I will not to do, that I practice."* This verse reinforces the concept that says our behavior is driven from the carnality in our subconscious mind and not our good intentions that we have in our conscious mind.

3) An Uncorrected Behavior from Our Past

Of the three root causes of glitches, this one may be the simplest to correct. It isn't necessarily tied to our *diseases of the soul* or our identity, so uprooting it can be much easier. Sometimes the adjustment comes with just recognizing it and choosing not to go down that path. To go back to the highway metaphor, we see that we have been taking the wrong offramp, so when we are triggered, we recognize what is happening and we choose not to take that exit.

Crocodile Tears

One friend of mine that I know very well used to have a behavior pattern that she repeated in certain situations around her family. I started to notice it when I would hear her talking on the phone to her family members. When she didn't get her way, she would revert to tears like a child trying to manipulate their parents. Except she didn't just do it with her parents, she did it with her siblings too.

For a season, she was a caregiver for my mother and lived about an hour and a half away. She had brought her newly purchased puppy to work a couple of days after she bought it. The ten-week puppy was full of energy and just wanted to chew on everything she could. The puppy was getting on the caregiver's nerves, so she called her father and asked him to come pick the puppy up. She wanted her father to drive an hour and a half to come pick up the puppy even though she would be getting off of work in six hours. He refused because he didn't feel like spending three hours of his day running an unnecessary errand. Puppies play hard but also sleep a lot; and he didn't see the logic in spending all that time, gas, and energy on picking up the dog when she could keep the puppy with her for a bit longer.

My friend acted like a three-year-old child with big old crocodile tears running down her cheeks, begging her father to come pick up the puppy. I couldn't believe what I was watching; she looked ridiculous. She wasn't crying like an adult. She looked like an adult who was trying to mimic a child crying. She wasn't intentionally trying to look and act like a three-year-old. I assume she cried the same way when she was a child and those same mannerisms carried over into her adult life. Her three-year-old temper tantrum behavior was never corrected when she was a child, she brought that behavior into adulthood.

I talked to her about her behavior that day, but she didn't see anything wrong with how she was acting because from her perspective, her behavior was normal. She didn't care that her request would be an imposition to her father and that it was selfish of her to even ask. She didn't see or care that she was using crocodile tears and emotional distress to try to manipulate her father.

One time, when she wasn't happy about something (I don't remember details of what it was), she tried to emotionally manipulate me the same way she used to with her family. She threatened to quit, but I didn't take the bait. I told her I won't be manipulated and if she wanted to quit, she was welcome to leave. She didn't quite know how to handle someone that didn't engage in an emotional way.

About a half hour after that conversation, she came back to talk to me and told me she didn't want to quit and asked if she could keep her job. I think it was around that time that she started to see her behavior and recognize it as a type of emotional manipulation.

Eventually she matured and much of that behavior subsided. A few years later, when she rented a room from me at a different house, a minor recurrence of that cry-baby manipulative behavior happened again when she was talking to a family member. I again brought it to her attention, and we talked through it. She wasn't trying to be manipulative. She wasn't trying to get emotional and cry. She just reverted back to that child-like behavior because it felt normal to her. That behavior had become an auto-response pattern in her family when she didn't get her way and her family played right into it. It became a glitch behavior that got repeated when it was triggered.

She really wanted to get married, and I told her she couldn't take that crocodile tears manipulative behavior into a marriage. She needed to figure out what triggers it and correct it. That whole next year was a year of seeking God and spiritual maturity. I haven't witnessed that behavior since then. She did find love and marry a wonderful Christian man.

Her manipulative crying is actually a common behavior. The only difference is my friend looked like a child when she cried to get her way. Millions of other women *adult-cry* to get their way, or they use passive-aggressive behavior or a bevy of other emotional responses. And before we blame women for emotional manipulation, men use emotions to get their way too. However, men usually use anger rather than crying to manipulate their family. Your loved ones shouldn't have to walk on eggshells for fear of provoking an emotional temper tantrum in you.

If you recognize emotional manipulation as an autopilot glitch in yourself, take measures to correct it. Don't give yourself a *free pass* with the rationalization that it is just your personality. It isn't a personality trait. It is emotional manipulation, and it is wrong.

The Trapped Mountain Lion

A person can have a traumatic event in their past where they reacted poorly to the situation. If that person doesn't regret their actions and see the error of their ways, they will most likely repeat their bad behavior in the future when similar situations arise. Even if the situations are different or they are not as drastic as the original trauma, the new circumstances can evoke similar emotions and trigger an autopilot response glitch. When that happens, the person will generally repeat their same negative behavior patterns.

A friend of mine that I have known for more than 20 years has one of those glitches. A big dramatic situation happened when she was approximately 20 years old. At the time, she lived with her sister and her sister's boyfriend. My friend and her sister's boyfriend fought all the time. There was always strife, yelling, and drama in their household. My friend's sister didn't want the drama anymore, so she told my friend to move out.

My friend was outraged that her sister chose her boyfriend over her. She felt utterly abandoned by her, especially since their mother had passed away. My friend was afraid because her shelter, her security, had just been stripped away so she lashed out with a mountain lion's fury. My friend completely vilified her sister and rehearsed every perceived wrong and called her every name in the book. She failed to recognize that her sister had already helped her in many ways, yet she labeled her sister as Satan's spawn. She refused to see the situation from any other perspective. She wouldn't acknowledge her own ugly behavior towards her sister. And she didn't recognize that the sister had a right not to want chaos in the house all the time. Instead, all she focused on was her sense of abandonment, how she had been wronged, and the perceived flaws of her sister.

Quite honestly, I don't blame the sister for asking her to move out. My friend had lots of great qualities, but she was also very argumentative, and she fought in a mean manner. Living with my friend at that time in her life was like living with a mountain lion that got its paw caught in a trap. When you try to help a trapped mountain lion, it still tries to attack you. My friend was so defensive that she always lashed out without regard for the wounds that she inflicted on others. She would provoke arguments and wouldn't let them die down. Her comments were beyond cruel when arguing and she went out of her way to verbally hurt people. She couldn't or wouldn't see how her actions impacted others. She only considered how she felt.

In the more than 20 years that I have known her, I have witnessed her repeat this behavior pattern maybe five or six times. It doesn't happen very often, but it can get triggered when she faces a housing issue, a major financial security issue, or a babysitting issue that she doesn't know how to fix. When a situation presents itself where it looks like the pillars of her stability can be removed, she is quick to pounce on the person who she thinks caused it or the one who could help her but chooses not to. It is a self-preservation attack. Regardless of how much that person may have helped her in the past, she will quickly turn on them and go into attack mode.

As I write this chapter, my friend is currently in mountain lion mode towards someone that is no longer helping her with personal issues. Maybe that is why I am talking about this trigger in the book right now, since I am witnessing it now.

I have watched and listened to her attack other friends of hers in the same way over the years when she has felt that they have failed her. There was even a season when she expressed this behavior towards me. In the late 2000's, she was renting a room from me, and we had a falling out. It was at a time when I was giving serious consideration to moving out of that house, which would obviously affect her living situation.

Instead of leaving on friendly terms, she spewed out ugly venomous comments about me to another roommate. I was shocked. I never said or did anything to purposely hurt her, yet I was being vilified and slandered to others. Through the years, I had given her so much and helped her beyond anything her family ever did for her as an adult. Yet, in her mind, I had turned into an evil person all the sudden.

I believe she consciously or subconsciously blamed me that she didn't have housing security. Even back then, I recognized that she was being triggered, and she was reacting emotionally the same way she did when she was 20 years old and facing possible homelessness. The level of anger and hostility towards me was way beyond what the situation should have entailed. She wasn't kicked out on the street. She didn't have to leave until I left. Yet emotionally, it triggered an old wound, and she responded to me in that old mountain lion manner.

I don't remember the exact timing, but I think we started talking again about a year after she moved out. When we reconnected, there was never a request for forgiveness for treating me in such an ugly way. And the reason for that – she didn't acknowledge her behavior as ugly or inappropriate.

I have counseled my friend with the mountain lion tendencies over the years about many different issues, but when it comes to this particular glitch, her ears are blocked, and she refuses any counsel. If I were to bring up the situation with her current enemy, it would only trigger her trapped mountain lion behavior. She rehearses the offense, exaggerates it, and just keeps lashing out ugly comments about the person.

There are some lessons we can take away from my friend's mountain lion behavior.

- A person can be fun and pleasant but then there are situations where they can flip a switch and turn irrationally mean and spiteful.
- The person that carries the most anger about a situation isn't necessarily the one that has been wronged. So many people think that if they scream the loudest that the other person has harmed them, that it makes them *in the right* and the other person *in the wrong*. The person carrying the biggest perceived wound, isn't necessarily the victim. Sometimes they are the villain in the story.
- Some people think it is acceptable behavior to be mean and spiteful in arguments. The winner isn't the one who hurts the other the most. The winner is the one who stands on the side of godly wisdom, grace, and temperance.

Closing Thoughts

Our glitches, our broken record behavior patterns, can be issues we are aware of or not aware of. But either way, they are flaws on our subconscious *hard drive* that cause us to repeat sinful and sabotaging thoughts or behavior patterns. Our glitches, whether they are caused by: 1) a *disease of the soul,* 2) our identity comfort zones or 3) a past behavior that we failed to correct, can cause significant damage and death to our relationships and opportunities. It behooves us to discover the ones that are active in our life and take measures to uproot and correct them.

Five

Pride

Let's face it. Most people don't see pride as that big of a deal. We have been conditioned to believe that pride is good. There are verses in the Bible that tell us that God hates pride. Yet, somehow, our culture doesn't view pride as a bad thing at all.

In fact, the word *pride* was negative and associated with sin until the 14th century when a positive connotation started to be associated with the word. Pride took on a whole new meaning, and the word began to be known as an emotional response or attitude of self-respect. The word *pride* is now associated with self-esteem, dignity, and honor.

According to Merriam-Webster, "Pride is a word that has had a number of changing meanings over its lifetime." I believe this may have been intentional. The kingdom of darkness could have orchestrated the change of meaning of the word.

The two possible reasons are:

- The Bible tells us that Lucifer was kicked out of heaven because of pride. Changing the meaning of the word may make people sympathetic to Lucifer and make it seem like God overreacted and was cruel.
- By giving the word a positive definition, it could covertly lessen the ugliness of the sin of pride. The human mind would subconsciously categorize it as good instead of an evil thing.

Why is Pride Bad?

- Pride is at the base of all *diseases of the soul.*

When I envision pride in our subconscious mind, I don't see it as one spot. I see it more like a giant spiderweb or root system that has strings in every corner of our subconscious mind. Our Adamic nature, our human carnality, has pride oozing out of us with almost every sentence. But it is so ingrained in us and intrinsic to our existence that we don't notice it.

With Satan's victory in the Garden of Eden, pride was sired into the blood line of humanity. When Adam and Eve sinned, they immediately hid from God. Hiding sin is a demonstration of pride. Adam and Eve also felt the need to hide their nakedness. Again, hiding, being self-conscious, and being embarrassed are all signs of pride. Carnality in the souls of mankind was birthed at the fall so, of course, humans would carry pride since it was grafted into us at Satan's victory. The children carry what is in the father. And Father Lucifer had pride so humanity, in our current state, carries pride.

We know that there are three primary colors, and a gamut of colors are created from combinations of those primary colors. Well, pride is like a primary color. All of the soul iniquities have traces of pride in them.

If we take measures to reduce our pride, then it will be much easier to see our other *diseases of the soul* and uproot them. As we discussed in the first chapter, pride is a major cause of blind spots. If we are ever going to attempt to uproot our soul iniquities, we need to start with pride.

• Pride Leads to Deceptive Thinking

The second reason why pride is bad is that it is a breeding ground for deception, as mentioned in the first chapter. Luke 1:51-52 says, *"He has shown strength with His arm; He has scattered the proud in the imaginations of their hearts. He has put down the mighty from their thrones, and exalted the lowly."* Pride causes imaginations of our hearts. And typically, the more pride a person has, the more delusional they are.

Lucifer is called the *Deceiver,* and when we are lifted up in pride, we give the reigns of our soul over to the enemy to plant all sorts of wrong thinking. I know that sounds a little dramatic, but it is true. Think of the proverbial angel sitting on one shoulder and devil sitting on the other shoulder in that idiom that dates back to the 16th century. It depicts how the devil tempts us to do wrong, while the angel on the other shoulder, encourages us to do good. Since pride blocks our discernment to hear from God, it is much easier for demonic suggestions to manipulate our pride and convince us to believe a lie.

In the first chapter of this book, I talked about how pride turns our heart cold, and I used the analogy of a pond being frozen over. That ice between our conscious mind and our subconscious mind blocks the Holy Spirit's voice that would normally travel from our spirit, through our subconscious mind, and then register it as a thought in our conscious mind. That metaphorical layer of ice causes our discernment to be impaired, which then causes us to have a hard heart so when we hear godly wisdom, we are more likely to reject it.

Layers of deception can cloud our perception of reality to the point that we are living in a false reality. Pride causes a person to believe their version of truth even if the real truth is completely different than their version.

- Pride is Hard to Recognize

Pride is also bad because it is hard to recognize and diagnose. Pride is like that octopus that swims along and as soon as it lands on some rocks, it changes its colors, so it looks like the rocks. It camouflages itself so we don't see it. If someone were to point out a prideful comment we made, it would be easy for us to justify and label it as something else.

When God told me I had pride, I searched the scriptures looking for clues. I kept trying to repent of it before I figured out how it had been manifesting in my life. Most of us assume pride is just arrogance, so we dismiss the issue when we don't see arrogant conceit in our behavior. For the most part, we are unaware that pride is like an octopus and has several tentacles of operation. Pride can have tons of mixture. Pride can have multiple shades of gray. It can be mixed with very good intentions, so it is hard to label it as black or white.

We can't say a quick "forgive me" prayer for pride and expect that to do the trick. We can't repent of something if we don't know what we did wrong. Just like a surgeon can't cut out cancer if he doesn't know where it is, we can't uproot pride if we haven't identified how it manifests in our life.

Here is a gardening analogy for pride. A manifestation of pride is like a weed in our garden. We go pull it out and we hope we got it all. Most likely there were small veins of the root that broke off and still remain underground and hidden. Those smaller veins can get larger and grow into new weeds. That is how it is with pride. We can uproot an ugly weed, but before we know it, another one has grown in its place.

However, the good news is, even if another weed (manifestation) pops up, we will know how to identify it. We may not be able to pull the entire root system of pride out with pulling just one weed. But the more pride weeds we get out of our life, the happier we will be and the more truth we will walk in. Some people live in a jungle of 8-foot-tall weeds of pride and don't even know it. They are so delusional, they think it's a manicured lawn.

- Pride Breaks God's Heart

God longs to have a living, breathing intimate relationship with every person on this planet. As previously mentioned, pride turns a person's heart cold towards God, and it weakens their discernment. As a result, they can't hear God's correction, affection, and direction. Pride makes a person think they don't need God, so they purposely make choices to avoid situations where they could have an encounter with Him.

Just like an earthly parent loves their child regardless of the situations they are in, that is how God loves us. And just like an earthly parent, if our child chooses to ignore us, it hurts us, it breaks our heart.

Pride Manifestations

Arrogant and Inconsiderate

When most people think of pride, they think of arrogance, haughtiness, or conceit. Arrogant people are so narcissistic that they view themselves as *the star of the show* and others are just supporting actors. They are so consumed their own wants, desires, and needs that they are completely oblivious to how their actions affect others. They usually only care how situations affect themselves. As time passes, they may ponder the feelings of others and how their actions impact others, but in real time, others are not a consideration.

Arrogance is very common in celebrities or sport stars who *hit it big* and are suddenly thrust into the spotlight. Other people treat them like a star, so they embrace the role, and they believe the hype about themselves. They are usually unaware or unconcerned about their character flaws, and they often treat others in demeaning or condescending ways.

Unteachable

Because prideful people have deceptive thinking, they are often unteachable. However, a high percentage of unteachable people are in-cognito. They have a smile on their face and can even nod their head in agreement. But internally, they reject the information that was given, and they believe they know more about the matter than the one that gave the new information or instructions.

I have witnessed this silent unteachable behavior in work settings. If an employee doesn't respect their supervisor or agree with what they are being told, they will simply tune them out. They will have outward agreement and compliance when the information is given. But in the break room, they will often criticize the supervisor or the new informa-tion to their close work friends. Rather than being open-minded and trying to glean value from the instruction, they will create reasons why it is bad information. They may even try to sabotage a new procedure, so they can validate to themselves and others that they knew best.

Reasoning

When a person reasons, they try to figure out the *whys and the wherefores.* Their deceptive thinking will not allow them to see their true motives that are driven by their soul iniquities, so they try to make sense of their behavior another way. Their reasoning allows them to come up with an explanation and justification for their behavior so it will make sense to them and to others. Reasoning also gives the person time to re-write history in their mind. Once a version of the incident emerges that paints them in a positive light, they rehearse that version in their mind until they believe it.

Manipulation

Manipulation can be a manifestation of pride. A prideful person that believes their way of doing things is the right way, may try to force other people to follow them by using manipulation as a means. Or they may try to manipulate others to get them to do things that cater to their selfish desires.

Anger

Anger can be a manifestation of pride in a few different ways. 1) Our pride can cause anger to arise because we believe our way is the right way and we feel angry if other people don't do things our way. 2) Anger can be used as a way to manipulate people and get our way. 3) Anger can be channeled at others when we may be the one that should be blamed. For example, we may yell and scream at other drivers when there is traffic, and we are running late. Well, we are the reason we are late, not the traffic. We should have estimated for the possibility of traffic and left earlier. Our pride usually tends to blame others rather than taking responsibility for our own lapses in judgement.

Lying

Telling *little white lies* can be a manifestation of pride and fear. What are we afraid of? Why are we trying to fix our problems in our own strength? Do we trust God or not? Every time we lie, we are demonstrating to God and to people that we don't trust God. We rely on our own creativity to get us out of tight spots or to make us look better in the eyes of others.

We don't lie. We embellish, exaggerate the truth, highlight the positive points, and overlook the negative ones. It is all done because our pride wants us to be esteemed more highly in the eyes of others.

Secrecy

We've been taught not to *air our dirty laundry* and keep family issues private. As a result of this type of secrecy, millions of Christians are captive to skeletons in their closet. They are prisoners of secret shame which is also a form of pride. Being ashamed of who you were or the mistakes you have made, denies the full power of Jesus' blood and His sacrifice. A humble person is transparent regardless of the reaction of others.

Secrecy caused by guilt, shame, and condemnation are tools the devil uses to weaken the body of Christ. We take away those tools when we expose the devil's lie. By keeping shameful things secret, we empower the devil to use them against us. When we expose our past and openly address the bondages, we are free from their hold. Secrecy is exalting the fear of man, over the fear of the Lord.

Shyness

Of course, shyness is more prevalent with certain personality temperament types. But shyness can be a form of pride. Like secrecy, it is exalting the fear of man, over the fear of the Lord.

If God tells someone to go witness to people at a store but they don't do it because of shyness, that person is disobeying God. They are putting themselves above obedience to God which equates to pride.

Embarrassment

The World Book Dictionary defines embarrassment as "to make self-conscious." *Self* issues are always rooted in pride. When you are self-conscious, you fear man's opinion. When you make a mistake or something private is revealed, there is a natural tendency to feel embarrassed. Pride and fear team up to form embarrassment. Embarrassment is rooted in a fear of rejection. We fear rejection if people see our mistakes, and we feel vulnerable if something private is exposed.

Self-Pity

Depression can be rooted in pride. While it is true that depression can be caused by demonic oppression or terrible losses in a person's life, it can also be caused by self-pity that is birthed out of a person's pride. Millions of Christians live their lives in self-pity. Self-pity, like all the *self* issues has pride as its root. Pride will always keep a person's focus on themselves. Narcissistic thoughts dwelling only on oneself can lead a person right into a *pity party*. When a person mediates and rehearses things they perceive to be wrong about their life, they are indulging in self-pity. However, considering and helping others who are less fortunate will remind you to *count your blessings* and to be thankful – which is the cure for self-pity.

Selfishness

The site www.Merriam-Webster.com defines selfish as: "concern excessively or exclusively with oneself or concentrating on one's own advantage, pleasure, or well-being without regard for others." Self, self, self = pride, pride, pride. Selfishness is our cultural *norm*. Everybody is *looking out for number one*.

Self-sufficiency and Self-Promotion

Many people don't recognize self-sufficiency and self-promotion as manifestations of pride, but they are. I used to know a woman that was very action oriented. She knew how to get tasks done. She was talented, creative, out-spoken, and she had a fix-it nature. When her actions got her in trouble, she was quick to take action to rectify the situation. She had flawed discernment. She was always rushing to solve a problem instead of waiting on God for wisdom. Her behavior demonstrated a lack of trust in God. She said she was trusting God to guide her, but her actions spoke differently.

We attended a large church at that time, and she was always promoting herself to church leadership. She was constantly trying to *buddy-up* to leadership so they would notice her calling and giftings. God knows how to promote a person without the person manipulating to *get their foot in the door.* 1 Peter 5:6-7 says, *"Therefore, humble yourselves under the mighty hand of God, that He may exalt you in due time, casting all your cares upon Him, for He cares for you."*

People-Pleasing

People-pleasing is similar to self-promotion, but it is a little more extensive. Self-promoting behavior basically focuses on impressing those in influential positions, whereas people-pleasing behavior is concerned about impressing everyone. A person's entire self-esteem is held together by the opinions of others. People-pleasing can be a manifestation of fear, but it is more commonly a combination of fear and pride.

People-pleasing is common among those with a non-confrontational personality. They are often riddled with insecurity, and they can be so afraid of losing relationships that they tolerate abuse. Because people-pleasers have a hard time saying "no", they often overcommit their time, energy, and money to various people and projects.

People-pleasing is a manifestation of pride because it places trust in people rather than God. People-pleasers reason within themselves that if they are only good enough or do enough, that people will like them and value them. But the truth is - people are fickle. They may love you one day and hate you the next. If your whole sense of self-worth is tied up in what others think about you, then it goes without saying, that the kingdom of darkness will use people to hurt you. Our value and our self-esteem must come from God and not man.

Testing God

We must always remember that there is a spiritual battle going on around us all the time. The devil doesn't have any new tricks; he just recycles the old ones. He tries to urge Christians to test God, just like he did with Jesus when He was in the wilderness. The devil tried to convince Jesus with scripture that if He jumped off a cliff, angels would come to His rescue (Luke 4:9-11).

The devil does the same thing today. He will whisper foolish, self-sabotaging instructions in our ear to try to masquerade as the Holy Spirit. The devil will appeal to our pride until the misdirected suggestions begin to make sense. Deceptive thinking can kick in and convince us that the misleading idea came from God.

We need to recognize this manifestation of pride for what it is. Too many Christians have destroyed their lives because the devil convinced them to take an action or not to take an action and tried to make the Christian think they were obeying God. They will quote a scripture like *"God will supply all my needs"* (Phil. 4:19) and think that means that they are special and don't have to work for a living. Occasionally, God will tell people not to go out and get a job but that is rare. If a person isn't doing what they should do in the natural to make an income, then they have to know with all certainty that they are obeying God's voice and not a demon that is trying to destroy their life. With major decisions that will impact your life, do not self-isolate. Seek godly counsel because as the Bible says in Proverb 15:22, *"There is wisdom in a multitude of counselors."*

Closing Thoughts

I believe pride is the only *disease of the soul* that everyone has. Since it was sired into humanity at the fall, it is part of our Adamic, carnal nature. Even though we all have it, we have it in different measures. A person with a reprobate mind, obviously has a ton of pride. While others who purposely take measures to root out negative thoughts and behaviors have far less pride in their subconscious mind.

Pride is a much bigger deal than most people realize. It affects our ability to recognize truth and causes us to embrace deceptive thinking. It impacts our relationship with God and can greatly weaken our discernment. The more pride we have, the greater the number of *diseases of the soul* we have and the larger those soul iniquities are. As we root out veins of pride, it will be easier to root out other iniquities.

Six

Fear

Fear is a liar and a thief. Fear has convinced people to do or not do so many things. If we stop to consider the affects fear has had on individuals, families, and countries, it would be alarming. Fear has started wars between countries and in families. Fear has ruined the lives of people who have lived in consent worry and anxiety. Fear has even driven some people to suicide or homicide. It has stopped some people from pursuing God-ordained relationships, educational advancements, business opportunities, and inventions. Fear has stolen many blessings that God intended His children to have.

There are five categories of fear. 1) safety fear, 2) comfort zone fear, 3) impending harm fear, 4) fear of evil fear, and 5) the *disease of the soul* of fear.

Safety Fears

I believe this category of fear is really the only good type of fear. We have or we should have an innate fear in us that tells us not to engage in dangerous activities. We shouldn't disturb a hornet's nest. We should fear walking on the ledge of a 20-story building. We should fear swimming with crocodiles. These are not irrational fears; these are normal life-preservation cautionary fears.

Comfort Zone Fears

I have talked a lot about comfort zones in this book. However, a person can be apprehensive of things they are not comfortable with and not have a stronghold of fear in their subconscious mind. Just because someone has a fear of public speaking, doesn't necessarily mean they have the *disease of the soul* of fear. With that said, a high percentage of people do have a stronghold of fear, a *disease of the soul* of fear, in their subconscious mind and they don't realize it. How do you tell? This chapter will help you evaluate your fear level so you can assess yourself.

Let's examine the fear of public speaking. Very few people are born with a natural boldness and fearlessness where they don't get nervous in front of crowds. Most preachers, actors, politicians, corporate managers, and others that are in positions where public speaking is required, started out being nervous about it. But, like with anything, the more we do something, the more comfortable we are doing it.

I will illustrate my own *stage fright* journey. In Junior High, I was in the musical, *The Music Man.* I was cast in the role of Mrs. Paroo, the female lead character's mother. I played a middle-aged Irish woman with an Irish accent. The accent came very easy to me; I was good at it so that was successful. However, the role also required that I sing a duet with Winthrop Paroo (played by Ron Howard in the original movie version of the play). Ugh. I had a soft soprano head voice, and the song required a loud, bold chest voice in a lower range than my singing range. I was completely terrified of the duet, but I did it. It turned out okay even though I dreaded it, and it caused me an abundance of anxiety.

When I first attended High School, I was very shy, both at school and in the high school group at church. One Sunday evening during my sophomore year, I was asked to read a story at the Sunday High School Bible Study meeting. I was asked to read the story by Lyle, a young man on the leadership team. Lyle knew that my older sister Stephanie taught speech, communication, and debate at Biola College, so he assumed I would perform a good dramatic reading of the story. I didn't. I was so nervous I could hardly get the words out. Yes, I had been in a musical production, but the play allowed me to prepare and rehearse my lines before I had to say them publicly. This was a *cold reading,* and I completely froze up and failed. I felt bad for the high schoolers there that night. I'm sure they were as uncomfortable as I was. It was ridiculous. I was so nervous I tripped up on all the words. It was torture for me, and it must have been torture for those that listen to me.

During my junior year, in spite of my tremendous fear, I decided to join the drama club. My first live show was a complete *train wreck.* The drama classroom was a small theater with a real stage, sound booth, lightening systems, and theater seating. A fellow student, Jeff, and I were supposed to do a scene from a Neil Simon play. During that performance, I kept walking off stage and leaving poor Jeff onstage all by himself in front of a live audience. Oh, it was an absolutely awful experience!

I was enrolled in the drama class; I couldn't just not show up anymore, so I continued and didn't give up. By the time I finished High School, I had been in more than 20 performances comprised of scenes, monologs, full plays, and musicals. At the end of my senior year, at the big theater department banquet with 50 to 60 students and their parents, I was awarded *Best Thespian* and *Best Actress* by the drama teacher.

And she even awarded me a "Bank of America Scholarship" plaque that was only given to one student per year.

After graduating High School, I choose a local community college that was known to have an excellent theater department. The college had a huge main theater, and they were holding auditions for *Rent*, the musical. I dreaded solos and duets, but I had done musicals before, so I was somewhat confident. When my name was called, I handed my sheet music to the pianist, and I walked out to the middle of the stage. The huge theater was black except for the spotlight that was on me and a small light on a clipboard that the director had in his hand. I attempted to sing but my nerves got the best of me. It was a complete fiasco. There was no recovery. I ended up saying, "never mind," and I ran off the stage.

I felt like dropping out of my classes and never showing my face on that campus again. But I attended that community college for a year and a half, and I actually did well in the acting and directing classes. The head of the fine arts department that covered drama, music, art, etc. ended up asking me to be a volunteer assistant in the Fine Arts office since I had secretarial skills. Soon after, the department chair awarded me a scholarship award that was only given to one person annually for the entire fine arts program.

Years later, I worked for a Fortune 500 computer manufacturer from 1988 to 1994 that had more than 4,000 employees at one time. I had to give presentations and speak in front of peers and management. After I was promoted to a manager, the level of management I had to interact with and give presentations to was significantly higher. At that point in my life, I was glad I had acting experience because it helped ingrain confidence in me so I wouldn't be as nervous with public speaking.

While working for that computer company and before I was promoted to a manager, I attended classes working towards a degree in business administration. One of the classes was a public speaking course. We had to give a presentation for our final that was video-taped. When I watched the video, I was horrified to see that I said, "um" after every sentence. That experience did two things. It made me more careful about saying "um" and it taught me that it was a good idea to film myself and watch it before delivering an important speech.

I had an intense spiritual encounter on my 30th birthday (12/12/94). As I was winding down for the night, I decided to read my Bible. A passage in the Bible literally glowed off the page and the presence of God filled my bedroom. That night I sensed God calling me into ministry. Even though I was enrolled in a Bible school at the time, I didn't know I was called to a pulpit ministry. I was strong administratively and in marketing, so I just figured I would work for God behind the scenes. I cried most of the night and didn't sleep all night. The primary reason was because the presence of God that had been in my room left an afterglow. And a secondary reason was I was grappling with the assignment God had just given me. By that point in my life, I had heard some amazing preachers and teachers. I wasn't at their level. I didn't think I could preach or teach like them. Additionally, prior to coming back to God, I had been backslidden for almost ten years and I was ashamed of my past. I didn't want to bring my shame and reproach on God by my sinful past.

Earlier that year in 1994, in the spring, after I had quit my corporate executive job but before I had surrendered my life to God, I took a stand-up comedy course at a local college. In 1996 and 1997, I did a handful of comedy gigs under an entity I formed called, "Stand-up for Jesus." A couple of those performances were at churches where I was able to do both a stand-up comedy routine and then preach a sermon. Was I looking for attention, fame, notoriety? No. In fact, my preference was not to have it. But I understood that God called me to teach and preach and the comedy opened some doors for me.

I attended Cottonwood School of Ministry from August of 1997 to June of 1999. In 2000, I taught a stand-up comedy workshop at Cottonwood. We then had a "Night of Stand-up Comedy" performance where I was the Master of Ceremony, and I performed the opening act. The workshop participates performed their stand-up routines and I had a professional comedian perform a longer set. I finished out the night by giving a 20-minute sermon geared towards evangelism. The night was enjoyable and memorable both for the audience and the performers.

From 2000 to 2007, I taught a weekly, lunch-time Bible study at my office. Work was extremely busy in that season of my life, so I didn't have a great deal of time to prepare for the Bible studies. I usually sought God the morning of the Bible study and then drafted bullet points and scripture references for a 20-to-30-minute sermon. My book, *Diseases of the Soul* was published in 2003 and with it came some itinerate preaching engagements and few TV and radio appearances. In 2007, I was the Master of Ceremony for the Miss Brea Beauty Pageant. I also did a stand-up comedy routine at that pageant. In addition to the Bible Studies and itinerate preaching in that season of my life, I was the president of a real estate company and a mortgage company, so I had to do some sales training meetings as well. The sheer number of times that I have spoken publicly has made me more confident and reduced my fear of public speaking.

Public speaking is one of the biggest comfort zone fears people have. As you can see from my journey, there were failures and successes. Failures should not be used as excuses, especially if that failure was in an area that God has highlighted to you as your assignment from Him. Like me, there are probably things that God has called you to do, that are outside of your comfort zone. Just because we are not comfortable with something, doesn't mean God gives us a pass to not do it. I have found in my life that as I have tried to walk in obedience to God, He has required me to do things specifically for the purpose of breaking fear from me.

Here are some takeaways from my experiences with combatting the comfort zone fear of public speaking:

1) Be Prepared. If I am prepared, meaning I have rehearsed notes to speak from or at a minimum, know the gist of what I will be talking about, I am much more comfortable. I have learned that the more prepared I am, the more comfortable I am. When stepping outside of your

comfort zone, don't set yourself up to fail; be prepared. Know the key points you want to address. There are some preachers that believe it is better not have anything prepared and just flow where the Holy Spirit takes them. That may be true for a very small percentage of preachers but not for the majority. It is a much better idea to have notes prepared and still allow the Holy Spirit to take you on *bunny trails*. I believe going on *bunny trails* with notes in front of you gives you more freedom in the spirit because the notes allow you not to be concerned about finding your place again after you have told the bunny trail stories. I have also seen several people improvise their eulogies at funerals. If your eulogy is scheduled and on the *Order of Service*, it should last between five to seven minutes. If it is an *open mic* sharing period at a memorial service, it should be no longer than three minutes. Having your message prepared allows you to regulate the timing of it. I have seen people distract from the memorial service when they didn't have their eulogy written down. I have witnessed eulogies that lasted less than a minute because the speaker couldn't think of what to say, and I have seen people drone on for 20 minutes without saying anything significant. When doing any public speaking, be prepared.

2) It's okay to fail. You can have humiliating failures and still recover and excel. At both my high school and college, I had horrible failures but came back and rose to the top. And although it wasn't mentioned previously, there was a time when I was new to stand-up comedy and I had a terrible audition. Yet, I went on to teach a workshop and host a stand-up show. Regardless of the failures – try again and again.

3) The more you step out of your comfort zone, the more comfortable you become. Between the years of 2000 and 2007, I would estimate that I taught, preached, or was interviewed approximately 450-500 times. The more we do something, the more comfortable we feel. Just because something is outside of our comfort zone today, doesn't mean it can't be in *our wheelhouse* down the road.

4) Don't Make Excuses. If we know God has tasked us with an assignment, obedience is not optional. God expects us to do everything we can to prepare for the assignment and to complete all the small steps along the way. The fruition of an assignment doesn't just fall out of the sky. God assignments require our participation and work. We cannot fool God with procrastination and excuses.

These same four points can be applied in any comfort zone fear. Let's look at a couple scenarios:

Getting a New Job

If you have been a housewife for 20 years and the idea of getting a job is way outside your comfort zone, follow these four things. 1) Be prepared for the job interview. Study interview techniques. Research the company you are interviewing with. Record yourself answering some typical interview questions. Watch the video and critique your mock interview then make adjustments accordingly. 2) You will have bad interviews, but don't give up. Keep at it. Don't allow the failures to discourage you. 3) The more interviews you go on, the more comfortable you will be and the better you will be at interviewing. When you are comfortable in an interview setting, it makes the person interviewing you comfortable and that can increase your chance of landing that job. 4) If you believe it is God's direction for you to have a job, then pursue it and don't make excuses.

Writing a Book

Maybe you feel like God wants you to write a book, but you have procrastinated because it is outside of your comfort zone. Do these four things. 1) Prepare yourself. Take a writing composition class so you can improve your writing skills if it is needed. Study the subject matter you want to write about. Seek God to find out specifically what He wants you to say. 2) Practice writing. Write articles and/or start to write some books. You will have some failures but its ok. Some writings that start out as a book may only end up being an article because you run out of content. That's okay, still write it. Don't over spiritualize it. Give yourself permission to fail a specific task but don't give up all together. 3) The more you write, the more comfortable you will be with it and usually the better you will become. Soon it will no longer be outside of your comfort zone. 4) "I don't have enough time," "I don't know how to get a book published," and "I don't have the money for publishing," are all excuses. Recognize them for what they are. Set a schedule for yourself and take an action each day, or week, or month according to the schedule you set for yourself. The tasks could be finalizing the out-line, writing a page, editing a chapter, researching publishing options, or really anything, as long as you are making forward progress.

Christians need to stop procrastinating God-given assignments just because they are out of our comfort zone. Don't get discouraged with failure. Don't assume everyone else is *just a natural*. Remember, what is uncomfortable will become comfortable the more you do it.

Impending Harm Fears

The third type of fear I want to talk about is the type of fear that happens when someone receives a negative report from the doctor, or something terrible has happened or may happen to you or your family. It is the kind of fear that can hit when you are suddenly laid off from your job and you don't know how you are going to pay the rent. It is the kind of fear that comes when your parent, child, or spouse has been in an accident. It's the fear that hits you when a doctor gives you a diagnosis you weren't expecting. It's the fear that your brain imagines the worst-case scenarios in situations.

There is a *faith switch* in these situations that will instantly put your mind at peace even though circumstances are not resolved. Isaiah 26:3 says, *"You will keep him in perfect peace whose mind is stayed on You because he trusts in You."* There is a metaphoric light switch of faith that is obtainable in these life crisis moments. The sheer shock of the bad news may take you a few days to get your bearings but there is a harbor of peace in the midst of a terrible storm.

Faith and fear are opposites. And it is in the fearful times in our life that we discover what our true faith level is in our subconscious mind.

Without going into all the details, there was a two-year period where I didn't have an income in the 90's. When I attempted to get a job, I felt constrained by the Holy Spirit not to do it. During that season, God was teaching me how to trust Him for finances. God needed me to see that He was trustworthy when I walk in obedience to Him and follow His promptings, even if they defied earthly wisdom.

I didn't ask anyone for a loan. I honestly don't know how I survived that long without getting evicted from the Irvine condo I leased. I don't recall programs like food stamps, welfare, or unemployment being options for me. Those programs are much easier to access today but they weren't even a consideration at the time. God told me to trust Him, I did, and He didn't fail me. The tiny amounts of money in my account would just last longer. A few times, money ended up in my account and I didn't know where it came from. As well, credit card companies would send me credit card limit increases without my request, and they would send me cash advance checks. People would approach me and just gift me money for no reason. I didn't tell my family that I was broke, partly because I didn't want to hear a lecture when I knew I was obeying God and partly because I wanted to demonstrate to God that I wasn't trying to manipulate them to give or lend me money.

I understand why God had that path for me. He had to get me to trust Him monetarily because trusting Him was necessary for the assignments that I was called to do. So many people say they trust God, until their car payment is late and then they panic. Trusting God means having peace in the midst of the storm. It doesn't mean that there will be no storm; it just means you are choosing faith over fear. True belief that we can trust God with our finances has to be established in our subconscious mind. The lack of fear, anxiety, and worry is proof that the light switch of faith has been activated in that area. God had me walk through that season because He needed me to learn how to trust Him for finances and to train my ear to discern His voice when it came to money matters.

During that unemployed season, I attended the Southwest Believer's Convention and Jerry Seville preached a message that birthed faith in my gut. He preached a message that said, "When you are at the end of your rope, let go and trust God." Suddenly, during that service, what I knew in my head dropped down into my gut. It was like the dark cloud of worry just lifted off me. Peace enveloped me. Faith for finances dropped from head knowledge to gut knowledge in my subconscious mind.

There are different types of faith and different types of metaphoric light switches. A person can have faith for finances but lack the faith for health and healing. If there is an accident or a sudden medical emergency, it is understandable to feel panicked, fearful, and worried. When it's an emergency, we do what we know to do. We try to make sure there is the best medical treatment possible, and we request other Christians to pray with us for healing and restoration.

What about when it's not a medical emergency but you have a negative doctors report? Most of the time we don't know how we would respond until we are in that situation.

In the summer of 2020, I had a new medical insurance plan. My new primary care doctor ran a number of blood tests, and one of the tests came back abnormal. My IGG level was elevated and my doctor referred me to blood cancer doctor with the concern that I may have multiple myeloma, which is a blood marrow cancer that doesn't offer a lot of treatment options.

There was a three-week period between my primary care doctor informing me I may have multiple myeloma and my appointment with the hematologist oncologist to review the results of additional tests. When I first heard about the possibility of cancer, I researched it on the internet. What I learned was not good. Multiple myeloma was one of the worst kinds of cancers you can have. And the first couple YouTube videos I watched on the IGG blood test and multiple myeloma didn't offer a lot of hope. They basically said you can have multiple myeloma and not have symptoms yet or you can be fully symptomatic and need to start chemo and radiation right away.

Surprisingly, I didn't react emotionally and just leaned into God to get direction. During that 3-week period, I prayed and asked God if I had cancer. I didn't get an answer. I just sensed God telling me to trust Him. I knew in my gut that I wouldn't die from cancer. But I didn't know if I would have to go through chemotherapy and lose all my hair. Fear tried to bombard me with questions like:

"Am I going to lose my job?"
"How would I survive financially if I do have cancer?"
"How would my daughter react to the news?"
"What would I look like bald?"
"Will I at least lose a bunch of weight going through chemo?"

I knew I wouldn't die from cancer because God had shown me a few visions of my future that hadn't taken place yet. And during that period, I kept being reminded of a prophetic word I received from a woman at a Woman's Aglow meeting approximately five years earlier. I had stepped out of the meeting to use the restroom. She followed me out to tell me that God had just spoken to her, and she was supposed to tell me that God was going to use me to impact millions of people's lives. That prophetic word resonated with me because it was something God had told me in the 90's.

I knew I would live but I didn't know if I would have to walk through a cancer battle or not. If I did have cancer, would I have a fast healing or a slow one with chemotherapy? The emotion of dread never came over me. I knew in my heart that God was with me, and He would hold my hand whatever the outcome would be. During that three-week period, I never prayed for healing. If I was sick, I knew that I would be healed so I wanted to wait until a diagnosis was made. I wanted the cancer to be documented, so God would get the glory for the healing.

I did know that healing and forgiveness seem to be linked together and that unforgiveness can sometimes block our healing. As I pondered that thought, I recognized that there was someone I was mad at. I felt hurt and betrayed by that person and anyone who knew the situation would agree that I had to right to be offended by his actions. At that point, I was ok with the idea of not having that person in my life. But God was telling me I needed to release the offense, so I did.

One day, maybe two weeks into the three-week waiting period, something happened that changed everything. I was an escrow officer at the time, and I had just gotten to work. When I went to grab my purse to put it under my desk, a yellow post-it note in my bag caught my eye. I pulled it out and read it. It was a note I had doodled the day before that said, "I will not fear" which was a reference to Psalm 23. When I saw that note, a light switch was flipped on inside of me. A righteous indignation rose up as I read the note for a second time out loud. I then told the devil, "You don't get to steal my joy!"

For whatever reason, my personality blossomed at that escrow company. I was known on my team to have a good sense of humor and even though we were busy, I usually lightened the load with humor several times a day. I enjoyed my job and my co-workers. When I read that note, I determined in that moment that I wasn't going allow fear and heaviness to rob me of my humor, peace, and joy.

Prior to that, I didn't necessarily feel fearful. I was leaning into God, and I knew He would be with me every step of the way regardless of what happened. But that morning, a deposit of fearlessness sunk into my gut. I can't say that I suddenly had faith healing because I didn't plan on seeking healing until after I heard the results of all the tests. However, since faith and fear are opposites, perhaps it was the same thing.

I ended up having a great day, full of laughs and friendly exchanges. That night when I got home, I looked up something on YouTube, and I discovered another video that talked about diagnosing multiple myeloma. Except this video gave a third option. It had the "you have the cancer but no symptoms" and the "you have the cancer and have symptoms and must start treatment right away" but it also had a third category which was "MGUS." Apparently, MGUS could be considered a pre-multiple myeloma diagnosis but roughly only 1% of MGUS people develop multiple myeloma annually.

When my appointment with the hematology oncologist (blood cancer doctor) finally happened, the doctor told me I was MGUS. This meant that there was "M" protein in my blood but not my urine. If it had also been in my urine than I would have had multiple myeloma. He said that MGUS is not an uncommon blood disorder, and it was estimated that approximately 3% to 5% of people have MGUS. He mentioned the standard protocol for his MGUS patients is for them to get tested two to three times a year to check certain markers. So, I don't have bone marrow cancer, praise God.

Fear of impending harm, either for ourselves or our loved ones, is something that most of us have faced in our life. I know from experience that when we first get a negative doctors report, we are shocked. Sometimes it takes a few days to reconcile in our mind the information that we just received. Oftentimes, when we get a negative report, we aren't ready to stand in faith right away because we are still numb from the news. I get it. I have been there a few times.

There have been plenty of times I have not sought God for healing, and I just relied on modern medicine. However, so far in my life, there have been three times where I have received healing using my faith. Two of those times, anger rose up in me because I knew the ailment was a direct attack by the devil. And the third time, I had a Rhema word from God that it wasn't His will for me to suffer. All three of those times, when faith rose up, fear diminished. So, our level of fear can be an indication if we have faith for healing deposited in our subconscious mind.

Most of the time, when Christians are diagnosed with an ailment, we don't seek healing from God. We just accept the sickness or ailment, and we rely on medications, surgery, or medical expertise to manage it. There is no shame in that. It is what most people do. It is just human nature. We don't *sweat the small stuff*. We, as Christians, usually only seek God for healing if: 1) we are in extreme pain, 2) the ailment can be fatal, or 3) the medical community doesn't have a remedy to fix the condition.

We accept and tolerate way more physical issues than we need to because the majority of the time we do not have a knowing in our gut that it is God's will to walk in health. We somehow subconsciously embrace that old false line that says, "If it is God's will to heal us, then He will do it." And even with Christians that believe they are supposed to be healed of a specific issue, most don't know for sure if they are supposed to: 1) attempt to receive healing by their faith, 2) get prayed for by the church elders, or 3) if God is planning on sovereignly zapping them healed at some point in the future. We are not sure of the "how" and "when," so we don't press in to receive our healing by faith.

When we get bad news, we need to evaluate ourselves. How much fear do we have? What scripture or memory is God reminding us of? If we have a prophetic word or a scripture, we need to hold to it. If we don't have a Rhema word or scripture when we have a new negative report, we need to get one and then meditate on it until it sinks down into our heart/subconscious mind. We also need to recognize that fear is our enemy in these situations, and we need to drive fear out.

Fear of Evil

Psalm 23 says, *"Yay, though I walk through the valley of shadow of death, I fear no evil."* How many Christians can honestly say that? When you encounter a demonic spirit, does fear rise in you or does faith rise in you?

I explore this topic in greater detail in my book entitled, *Real Stories of Angels, Demons and the Supernatural.* The book details the experiences I have had with angels, demons, and the supernatural.

As previously mentioned, demons thrive when fear and ignorance are present. They are like cockroaches; as soon as the light is switched on, they stamper and flee. I highly recommend that Christians learn about the spirit world and know how to cast out demons. Hosea 4:6

says, *"My people perish for lack of knowledge."* If people live in fear and ignorance of the spirit world, the kingdom of darkness can destroy their life. All Christians should take an active role in dispelling fear and ignorance, so God's will can be done on Earth.

Kenneth Hagin wrote a small book called, *The Believer's Authority* which teaches Christians how to use their authority in the spirit realm. In the book, he uses this illustration: There is an intersection with a police officer standing in the middle of the street directing traffic. A big truck comes to the intersection and stops because the police officer has his hand up to stop. That truck obeys the officer's signal. Why? Because that officer carries authority. That is how it is in the spirit realm. A truck may have more physical power than the police officer and could easily run the officer over. But he doesn't because he obeys authority. Demons may have more spiritual power than humans, but Christians have the authority that Jesus gave to us.

Luke 10:19 says, *"Behold I give you power to tread on serpents and scorpions."* which is symbolic for demons.

1 John 4:4 says, *"Greater is He that is in us, than he that is the world."*

Proverbs 28:1 says, *"The righteous are as bold as a lion but the wicked flee when no one pursues."*

And let's not forget the Great Commission. Mark 16:17-18 says, *"And these signs will follow those who believe: In My name they will cast out demons, they will speak with new tongues; they will take up serpents; and if they drink anything deadly, it will by no means hurt them; they will lay hands on the sick, and they shall recover."*

We are in a season that all Christians should understand their spiritual authority and should walk in it as Jesus commanded us to do. We are God's ambassadors on Earth, and He has told us that it is our job to cast out demons and reverse the wiles of the kingdom of darkness. But we can't do that if we fear demons.

The *Disease of the Soul* of Fear

The final type of fear I want to address is the *disease of the soul* of fear. The question could be asked, "How can we distinguish between comfort zone fears and a *disease of the soul* fear?" Below are some questions we can ask ourselves that may help bring clarity:

- Do you have any phobias?
- Are there things that terrify you that don't bother other people?
- Was there an event in your past that may have scarred your psyche and birthed a root of fear in you?
- Could fear be a *generational curse* in your family?
- Has God given you assignments, but you haven't done them because of fear?
- Are there actions you take or don't take that others don't understand?

Diagnosing a root/spot/cancer of fear in someone's subconscious mind may be a challenge because, oftentimes, the person won't see it. It is their normal way of life, and it doesn't seem strange to them.

I had dinner with a very nice Christian woman who was an acquaintance from church. During dinner, God told me the woman had two *diseases of the soul*: pride and fear. The pride was pretty easy to see. All she did was talk about herself. I'm sure she probably wasn't aware of how narcissistic she came across that night. But it also became evident that she had a root of fear as well. When I asked her about the jobs she has had in her life, she seemed to get a little defensive and said she had never been employed. She had always been a wife and mother. She was older and an empty nester, but she looked great. She was attractive, dressed well, and seemed smart. I have interviewed hundreds of candidates for jobs over the years and she seemed very employable. At that particular time, her husband's job was volatile, and he wasn't bringing in very much money. I didn't understand why she didn't try to get a full or part time job. She just made excuses as to why she was needed at home.

What this godly woman has done is what so many other godly people have done. They have embraced the Bible verse Philippians 4:19, which says, *"And God shall supply all your needs according to His riches in glory by Christ Jesus."* They lean in on and rely on trusting God for their finances. And I get that. I did that for a two-year season that I mentioned earlier in this chapter. However, my *trusting God for finances* season wasn't because I was afraid of working. I had been a successful corporate executive by that stage of my life. This woman had a blind spot of fear, and she couldn't see that her inaction was because of a *disease of the soul* in her subconscious mind.

Isaiah 1:19 says, *"If you are willing and obedient, you shall eat of the good of the land."* Most Christians haven't been obedient to God's direction in their lives and that is why a lot of them lack in the financial arena. Fear has caused them not to obey logic which would tell them to go get a job or get a better job. They haven't been obedient because they haven't allowed their ear to hear God encouraging them to take steps to excel in business. Just like that woman shut me down with her rehearsed excuses, that is what a large percentage of people have done when God has nudged them in a direction. Their hidden fear has caused them to shut down and makes excuses.

2 Timothy 1:7 says, *"For God has not given us a spirit of fear but of power, love, and a sound mind."* Let's dissect that verse a little. Would it be incorrect to say that if a person has a strong root of fear in them, they may be weak in their power, love, and soundness of mind?

Spiritual Power

Biblical faith is believing God's word about a situation. Fear is doubting God's promises and it is allowing our emotions to agree with the devil's plan. Well, when we agree with the devil's agenda, we lack spiritual power.

James 1:6-7 says, *"But let him ask in faith, without doubting, for he who doubts (fears) is like a wave of the sea driven and tossed by the wind. For let not that man suppose that he will receive anything from the Lord (8) he is a double-minded man, unstable in all things."* So, fear and doubting result in weak spiritual authority.

Does God still hear our prayers if we are fearful? Yes, of course. God will still be our salvation in times of trouble. But in *taking new ground* prayers and declarations, we will lack power when fear is in us.

Love

When we allow our fear to rule us and control us more than our love for God and obedience to Him, then our love level gets suppressed. The same is true in relationships. If a wife has a fear of leaving the house, she puts that fear above her love for her husband because her husband wants her to go places with him. Rather than being motivated by love; she is motivated by fear.

Sound Mind

When we fear, we often let that emotion overrule rational, logical thoughts. As of this writing, my daughter has a huge fear of bugs and spiders. That is understandable if she were afraid of dangerous spiders. But my daughter freaks out and screams if she sees a fruit fly, moth, or common housefly. Recently I came home, and my daughter was hiding in her room because she saw a fly in the kitchen. That is not logical! It doesn't matter how many times she is told that the fly can't hurt her, her fear triggers complete terror in her mind.

Fear is an unseen bondage. We are a society of circus elephants. A baby circus elephant is taught to stay in the pen by chaining its ankle to a peg, so it knows not to go beyond the length of that chain. When circus elephants are grown, they still stay chained to the peg. They don't realize they have the power to pull the peg out of the ground with one easy tug. We are like the grown circus elephants. We obey limitations that we don't have to obey. We have the capacity to do so much more than we think we do. We, as a society, are so used to the limits we have placed upon ourselves, that we don't dare reach past those limits. We will live in what is familiar, even if God has a much better path for us.

Fear Manifestations

Worry

Worry is one of the most common manifestations of fear. The problem is that people don't label worry as worry. They say things like, "I can't stop thinking about that situation." Well, if you are continually thinking about a situation, you are worrying about it. Rehearsing a situation over and over again in your mind is worrying.

Stress

Not all stress is rooted in fear, but it can be rooted in fear. Stress can be a more subtle form of worry. Stress manifests when a person becomes overwhelmed by too many concerns. Some of those concerns are projects on their "to do" list but other concerns are their fears. Stress can manifest when a person fears the loss of possessions, the loss of status or position, loss of respect, loss of love in a relationship, loss of control and so forth.

Embarrassment

Embarrassment is usually a mixture of pride and fear. A fear of rejection can cause the embarrassment.

Shame

Shame is a painful feeling of humiliation or distress caused by the consciousness of wrong or foolish behavior. It can bring a loss of respect or esteem where a person feels dishonored, disgraced, and degraded. It is worrying about the opinions of people rather than obedience to God. Fear of shame can cause a person not to go forward to an altar call when the pastor calls out an issue that they struggle with.

Anger

We all know that when an animal is trapped in a corner, it can lash out. Many people lash out in anger when they are afraid. Fear causes adrenaline to be released and it is often channeled into anger.

A past roommate of mine used to always respond in anger whenever we pranked her. Whether it was a fake snake by the trash can, a fake cockroach in the cabinets, or jumping out at her from behind a door, her reaction was the same. There would be a scream of fear, followed up by anger. When her adrenaline had subsided, she would then laugh at her reaction and then swear revenge. It was interesting to me that her auto-response to fear was always anger.

Controlling Behavior

When someone is a *control freak*, it is usually because they have a root of pride and fear. It's pride because they think they have the right solutions. And its fear because they are not willing to trust others. They fear others will do things wrong.

Secrecy

People with a root of fear often try to hide certain details and actions from others. A wife may hide purchases from her husband for fear that he would overact. An employee may hide their mistakes from their boss for fear of looking bad. A child may hide their grades from parents for fear their electronics could be taken away.

Lying

Lying can just be a deeper level of secrecy that is rooted in fear. Fear can cause people to misrepresent the truth, so their secrets won't be revealed. Their fear convinces them that lying is better than revealing the truth.

Overly Protective

A mother can be overly protective of her children because she fears they will get hurt. An athlete can be overly protective of their sports gear because they fear them being lost or damaged. Being overprotective can manifest in many ways but it is usually fear disguised as being careful.

Spiritual Deafness

I touched on this manifestation when was talking about the woman I had dinner with that wouldn't consider getting a job. Her response to getting a job was so rehearsed and embedded into her identity that she had become spiritually deaf in that area.

Another situation happened many years ago. I had a nice, Christian roommate and God told me in January that she was supposed to move out in March. God told me there was an opportunity coming her way, but it was dependent on her moving out of my home. I told her that and gave her an eviction notice for March. I told her in January, but February and March rolled by, and she didn't attempt to look for alternative housing. She had a good job and a nice demeanor; she would be a desirable renter. Then, sometime in April she started looking for somewhere to rent. I reminded her that the word was for her to move in March. I told her there is no sense of urgency to move in

April because the window of opportunity was in March. She assumed I "evicted" her because I was trying to get rid of her. But that wasn't the case. A few months later she lost her job. I believe the opportunity that God had for her with a new housing situation also had a new career opportunity.

You may ask, why would God tell me to tell her to move out in March? I believe God had been trying to talk to her about moving but her ears were closed to the idea because of her fear of change. Fear can close a person's spiritual ears.

Fear of Rejection

None of us like rejection and many of us have a deep-rooted, sub-conscious fear of rejection. Many people are so starved for love that they do things they shouldn't do. Some will live in abusive situations because it is better than being alone. They will go out of their way to please people because they don't want to be rejected.

Most people who have a root of rejection are unaware of it because it operates in their subconscious mind. They assume their behavior is normal. In most cases, they don't understand the root, so they justify and rationalize the behaviors. Their behaviors, thoughts, and actions make sense to them because it's all they know.

Closing Thoughts

There are different categories of fear. The categories are: 1) safety fear, 2) comfort zone fear, 3) impending harm fear, 4) fear of evil fear, and 5) the *disease of the soul* of fear. There are different ways to handle the different types. We need to understand that fear is not our friend. Fear can rob our life and cause us to live below the life God wants us to have.

Seven

Unforgiveness/Offense

The soul iniquity of unforgiveness and offense is one of the most common soul diseases people possess. I would estimate around 75% of people have this dark spot in the soul. That is not to say that the other 25% don't occasional get emotionally wounded and have a hard time forgiving someone. But the difference is when the 25% people release it, they release it. They don't think about it anymore and oftentimes forget the details of the offense over time. I've noticed that people with the *disease of the soul* of unforgiveness don't forget the offensive issue as easily. People in that 25% group, depending on the details of the incident, usually forget the issue within hours, days, or weeks. If it was an emotionally traumatic event, they may remember it for a longer period of time, but the incident isn't something they rehearse in their mind. If they were asked about the offense a year after they forgave the emotional wound, some of the details of the incident would be a bit fuzzy in their memory because they hadn't thought about it in a long time.

Whereas a person with a root of unforgiveness, can usually remember most of the details of the offense and then even create some additional fabricated details that strengthen their right to be mad or hurt.

It's a Big Deal

I would assume that most of the people reading this book are spiritually mature Christians. I would assume you, the reader, are aware that forgiveness is a big deal to God.

Colossians 3:13 says, *"Bearing with one another, and forgiving one another, if anyone has a complaint against another, even as Christ forgave you, so you also must do."*

Matthew 6:12 in the Lord's Supper, Jesus says to pray that God will forgive you as you forgive others.

Luke 6:37, *"Judge not, and you shall not be judged. Condemn not, and you shall not be condemned. Forgive, and you will be forgiven."*

You would think most Christians are familiar with these scriptures. Yet, I am so surprised when I come across a truly bitter Christian that thinks they have the right to not forgive someone. Do they not know that the Bible says they won't be granted forgiveness by God if they are carrying unforgiveness in their heart? God has been so gracious to us, but we are going to have a different measuring stick for others?

Matthew 6:15 says, *"But if you do not forgive men their trespasses, neither will your Father forgive your trespasses."*

Mark 11:25-26 says, *"And whenever you stand praying, if you have anything against anyone, forgive him, that your Father in heaven may also forgive you your trespasses. But if you do not forgive, neither will your Father in heaven forgive your trespasses."*

Two people come to mind when I talk about this subject. They both have raging hostility towards the people that they think have done them wrong. Yet, both of them have some of the ugliest behavior I have witnessed from human beings. They have been mean, spiteful, and downright evil towards others in their thoughts, words, and actions. They project evil intentions onto others whose outward sins pale in comparison to their own. And yes, their pride has caused deceptive thinking to convince them that the vile imaginations of their hearts are true.

Both of these people proclaim that Jesus is Lord of their lives. Really? Jesus says in John 14:15, *"If you love Me, keep My commandments."* And the Bible clearly commands us to forgive.

Forgiveness and Healing

It has been my observation that there seems to be a connection between forgiveness and healing. This concept isn't necessarily doctrine; it is just my observation. There are verses that imply the two are connected like James 5:16. It reads, *"Confess your trespasses to one another, and pray for one another, that you may be healed. The effective, fervent prayer of a righteous man avails much."* The assumption is that if someone is confessing their wrongdoing, they are asking for forgiveness and then the verse implies it opens the door for healing.

As we read the Bible, we will see that whenever the word "forgiveness" is mentioned, the word "healing" is usually within a verse or two of it and vise versa.

2 Chronicles 7:14 says, *"If My people who are called by My name will humble themselves, and pray and seek My face, and turn from their wicked ways, then I will hear from heaven, and will forgive their sin and heal their land."*

Psalms 103:2-3 says, *"Bless the Lord, O my soul, and forget not all His benefits: Who forgives all your iniquities, who heals all your diseases."*

When Jesus healed the paralytic man in Matthew 9:2, He said, *"Son, be of good cheer; your sins are forgiven you."*

To my knowledge there isn't a scripture that specially says unforgiveness blocks healing. But we do see evidence of it in medical science.

There are numerous medical and scientific studies that show a person's emotional health can have a serious effect on their physical health. Negative emotions like anger, revenge, and anxiety can greatly weaken the body's immune system and make them more susceptible to cancers, strokes, heart disease, and other ailments. We do know the opposite is true as well. When a person has joy, laughter, peace, and contentment in their soul, their natural immunity is strengthened.

The Bible supports this as well. Proverbs 17:22 says, *"A merry heart does good like a medicine."*

We understand that we don't create doctrine based out of our personal experiences and theories. However, it makes sense that unforgiveness may sabotage healing if we look at how people receive supernatural healing. We acknowledge healing can come one of three ways. 1) God can supernaturally and sovereignly zap us healed. 2) We can have a James 5:14 healing, where the elders of the church pray healing over us. And 3) We can receive healing by our faith where our knowledge that God wants us healed goes from knowing it in our conscious mind to knowing it in our subconscious mind.

When a person has unforgiveness, there is an area of the heart that is hard, cold, and nonreceptive to the voice of the Holy Spirit. They have either consciously or subconsciously rejected God's command to forgive. God is God and He can do whatever He wants. But is it logical to expect God to zap us healed when we are openly defying His commands to forgive and love others? As well, it is difficult for us to attain faith in our subconscious mind when we pridefully think our offense is justified. Do you remember the analogy of the frozen pond and how our pride can block faith from sinking down into our subconscious mind? Well, unforgiveness has lots of traces of pride in it and it becomes difficult to get those mustard seeds of faith down into the soil of our subconscious mind when we hold onto offenses.

I have seen people receive their healing when they release offenses and forgive. Back in the early 2000's, a friend of mine asked me to go with her to pray for her cancer-ridden mother who was in the hospital.

When we got to her hospital room, I was told that she had several cancer tumors throughout her abdominal cavity and doctors told her it was pointless to try and operate to remove them because there was so much of it. The woman was a good, godly woman. She understood faith and the prayer of healing. As I was praying for her, I had a *word of knowledge*. The Holy Spirit told me to tell her, "Your healing will come when there is forgiveness." She nodded her head in agreement and thanked me for coming. About a week later, I heard from my friend. She told me that her mother had received her healing and was completely cancer free. She said the doctors didn't understand what happened. My friend's mother, recognized the area of unforgiveness, purged it, and received her healing, just as the word of knowledge told her.

In another situation like the one mentioned in the above paragraph, a woman approached me and asked me to pray for her because she had heart disease. As I was praying, I sensed the spirit of God telling me that the healing of her physical heart was tied to the healing of her emotional heart. As I continued to pray for her, God showed me issues and hurts from her past that He wanted to heal. God also revealed to me that she was carrying unforgiveness that was blocking her healing. After I finished praying for her, we talked. She recounted a major tragedy in her life that had happened years prior. She said she knew exactly who she was holding unforgiveness towards and she seemed appreciative for the insight.

I believe offense can block healing. I'm sure it isn't always the case. But if you are seeking healing, I would encourage you to take an inventory of possible offenses you may be carrying in your heart and do your best to release them.

Unforgiveness Towards Self

Most of us have experiences in our past that we regret. However, some of us have sins, mistakes, or other actions in our past that have marked us. Our own foolishness or lapses in good judgment may have caused great harm to others. Some of us may even have subconsciously embraced the idea that we don't deserve forgiveness. It is not uncommon for people to subconsciously sabotage their success in life because of hidden, undiagnosed unforgiveness towards themselves. I have known people that wasted their life living in the regrets of their past.

If you don't forgive yourself, you are telling God that the sacrifices Jesus made on the cross weren't big enough to cover all your sins. God's grace is sufficient to cover your mess ups. You need to extend the same grace towards yourself.

If you aren't sure if you are holding unforgiveness towards yourself, reflect on the mistakes, disappointments, or wrong turns you have made. If there is an area of regret, ask God to reveal to you if you are holding unforgiveness towards yourself. If you are, repent and ask God to help you fully release it. We, as Christians, don't get the option to select which sins we get to keep. For some of you reading this book, God is telling you it is time to forgive yourself.

If there is an area of active sin in your life and that is the area that you don't forgive yourself from, then you would obviously need to address the root sin issue first before addressing self-forgiveness. But whatever the area is, know that God stands ready to help you with it.

With that said, too many people are carrying around guilt, regret, shame, and unforgiveness that needs to be released. If God can forgive you, then take His lead and forgive yourself.

The Forgiveness – Offense Connection

When I talked about the soul iniquity of unforgiveness, I link it together with offense although they are slightly different. Yes, unforgiveness is when you get offended by somebody. But the connection is like stages of cancer. Unforgiveness is like early stages of cancer and the spirit of offense is like stage 4 cancer. So, it's the same cancer but just at different levels of advancement. Unforgiveness is a wounded area in the subconscious mind. But when it turns ugly, it becomes a spirit of offense. Offense is the mean side of unforgiveness. When a person's pride goes unchecked, their deceptive thinking links arms with their root of unforgiveness and the manifestations can turn more hostile, toxic, and delusional.

Unforgiveness/Offense Manifestations

Ignores a Person

A beginning stage of unforgiveness can be to simply ignore the person who has harmed us. Most of us have heard people say, "I forgive them, I just don't want to be around them." Wanting to avoid a person can be a sign that there is unforgiveness towards them. We don't have to be close friends with an abusive or carnal person but if they were our friend before, suddenly labeling them as abusive or carnal may demonstrate unforgiveness.

Getting Feelings Hurt

Some people are wounded souls that get their feelings hurt too easily. Of course, everyone is hard-wired differently and some people are more sensitive, but at some point, allowing ourselves to get triggered with offense is a choice.

Remembers Everything

I mentioned at the beginning of this chapter that a person with a root of unforgiveness usually remembers details of offenses where others don't. As an illustration, a person with a soul iniquity of unforgiveness can remember that Suzy Baker pulled her hair in the fourth grade. Susie said, "Your hair is too curly. Do you stick your fingers in a light socket every morning to get it like that?"

People in the 25% group that don't carry offense, don't remember minor offenses. They barely remember significant events, much less frivolous comments made by another kid decades ago. But people with a root of unforgiveness tend to remember most of the negative things that were said and done to them.

Manipulation

Some people in relationships keep a mental score board of wrongs done to them. They use their spouses' mistakes to make their husband or wife feel guilty and may try to manipulate them with that guilt. If they caught their spouse in a lie years ago, they may bring it up in arguments to get the upper hand. If one of them caught the other flirting with someone else, the wounded spouse may mimic emotions of betrayal to get their way. Some wrongs will never be forgiven or forgotten; especially if those grievances can be used to their advantage.

Anger

Anger can be a manifestation of several different *diseases of the soul.* It can be an expression of unforgiveness, pride, jealousy, prejudice, rebellion, or greed. The World Book Dictionary defines anger as "the feeling one has towards something or someone that hurts, opposes, offends or annoys."

If someone offends us, the knee-jerk reaction is to get angry. However, if that anger emotion doesn't subside after a bit, it could be a sign that there is a spirit of offense within a person. If the anger doesn't taper off, it could demonstrate that the person is starting to stew over the offense. Usually, once the person has worked themselves into a tizzy, their pride kicks in and they can allow deceptive thinking to distort some of the facts of the incident.

Self-Pity

When someone is holding onto unforgiveness, it is very common for them to have different degrees of self-pity. They will often nurse their emotional wound and allow the details of the incident to get distorted in their memory. When they talk about their grievance, they want others to agree with their offense and validate their right to be wounded. Depending on the degree of self-pity, the offense can be used as an excuse to disconnect and not to engage in normal activities.

Victim Mentality

A victim mentality is similar to a pity-party, but a pity-party is usually temporary. A victim mentality can happen when a person fully embraces the delusion that their problems are always someone else's fault. They fail to see their role in their circumstances and will place the blame on other people or external influences. They often have a sense of entitlement and think people, companies, or the government owes them.

Years ago, a woman wrote me a nine-page letter because she wanted me to give her money or help her find a ministry or church that would pay her bills. She wrote about everything that was wrong in her life. From her viewpoint, bad things just kept happening to her. She was oblivious to the fact that it was her decisions that put her in the position she was in.

It has been my observation that a large percentage of homeless people have a victim mentality. Many of them don't take any responsibility for their circumstances. Most of them refuse to acknowledge that it was their actions or inactions that caused them to be in their current state.

Having a victim mentality isn't limited to the homeless. While most homeless people have a victim mentality, many functioning members of society can embrace the victim mindset, as well. They take no personal responsibility for the setbacks and failures they have had. Like the pity-partyers, they use the perceived wounds inflicted on them by others and their bad luck as excuses not to strive for success.

Things Bug Them

This manifestation is one that shows up in more than one soul iniquity. When someone holds unforgiveness, they are miserable. If they see someone having fun, succeeding, or happy, it can make them simmer in their own man-made misery. Even the smallest things can bug them. They are often edgy and annoyed. They want others to hide their happiness and act despondent because they are unhappy.

Project Motives

Projecting motives is starting to get into the uglier side of offense. When unforgiveness and pride have both gone unchecked in a person's heart, it is easy for them to create false beliefs in their imagination. They will assume their theories on the motives of others are true and can believe a false narrative.

In the late 90's, I attended a large church. The pastor had just finished preaching a message about forgiveness and he dismissed the service. As I was heading towards the exit, a woman I hardly knew approached me and told me she wanted to talk to me. I said "sure," and we sat down in a quiet area in the sanctuary. She told me that God spoke to her during the service, and she wanted to "clear the air" between us. I didn't know what she was talking about. She started discussing a falling-out that she and I apparently had about a year earlier. She said one Sunday night in the crowded foyer, our eyes met, I gave her a dirty look, and started walking in a different direction. She said I snubbed her, but I had no memory of the incident. Most likely, when the hostile clash occurred, I was probably zoned out, thinking about something else, and not paying attention to the people around me. This woman wasn't even on my radar, but I had become her arch enemy. She commented that we had both been giving each other dirty looks for a year but I was completely oblivious to the feud I was supposed to be in. She believed I was thinking all kinds of evil towards her because she was thinking that towards me, and it was all in her imagination.

A person with a root of offense concocts false realities in their minds all the time. The ugly, diseased, tumor of offense in their soul convinces them of things that are just not true. The next time you or someone you know comments on what they think another person is thinking, remind them that they do not have that superpower.

Re-Write History

A person with an infected spot of offense in their subconscious mind can re-write history on a regular basis. They dwell on their offenses, and they rehearse them over and over in their mind. They usually embellished details that are in their favor, leave out other key pieces of information, and create aspects to fit their side of the story. They meditate on the false information so much in their mind, that they embrace that version as the truth.

As I have mentioned, my brother Ken had a big root of offense. He could get bent out of shape about almost anything. Ken lived at our parents' house, where I also lived for seven years when I was the trustee of the family estate. One of my mother's caregivers, Sue, had several of her shirts hanging on the door frame of an extra bedroom that was only used for storage. Ken wanted to get into that room to get something out of the closet. He asked Sue to move her shirts so he could get in the room. Sue said, "sure, give me a couple minutes." He immediately came to me and blasted Sue. He said she was controlling and on a power trip for not moving her shirts the very instant he asked.

A few minutes later, after Sue had moved her shirts, she came to me and mentioned that the reason she didn't move the shirts right away was she wanted to move something in the room before Ken went in there. Apparently, when she and I were in that room sorting things, I had casually commented on something saying, "better not let Ken see this." I don't even remember what the item was. I don't think it was anything significant. But Sue had wanted to get into the room to move it before Ken went in there, so it didn't trigger his erratic behavior. But instead, her request for a couple of minutes triggered an outburst.

Over time, that ten-second conversation got twisted and magnified in Ken's mind. Details were added that weren't real. He turned something that wasn't even a speedbump into Mount Everest. Whenever he was frustrated at me, he would bring up Sue and how I was a terrible house manager because I hired evil and controlling caregivers. He even accused Sue of stealing our father's gun and a box of rare coins, so hiring thieves got added to the venting rampages. Bear in mind, Sue was a very strong Christian woman with impeccable morals. I had known her for several years, and she even rented a room from me for a while at a different house. She wouldn't steal gum if it accidently got left in her cart and wasn't rung up with her other groceries. Yet, Ken had turned her into the anti-Christ in his mind because his spirit of offense was good at re-writing history.

Vows Revenge

If a person plots revenge, then their cancer of offense is in full stage 4 cancer mode. It has mutated and spread. Not only has the person allowed their deceptive thinking to get out of control, but they are also demonstrating that they are at the point of acting on it. They are considering doing harm to another person because of what they believe the motives of the other person are.

There are distinct reasons God tells us that vengeance belongs to Him in Romans 12:19. One of those reasons is that it is God who truly knows the motives of a person's heart. He knows the details of the situation that we do not know. However, someone with a soul cancer of offense somehow thinks they know all the details, motives, and solutions to settle the matter. Vanity, pride, unforgiveness, and evil – that is what vowing revenge is at its root. A person that plots revenge is really the person that needs to be corrected by God.

Closing Thoughts

Unforgiveness is one of the more common *diseases of the soul* so consider the possibility that you have it. The problem with unforgiveness is the carrier usually views themselves as the victim. And yes, you can be a victim from what you have suffered and endured. However, to continue to carry unforgiveness is a sin. If we start treating it like the soul iniquity that it is, then we will have more motivation to uproot it out of our subconscious mind. Just because it is a pet sin that most people carry, does not mean that we should allow it to damage our relationship with God and those that are close to us. Remember, unforgiveness is a very big deal to God.

Eight

Jealousy/Envy

Jealousy is another common *disease of the soul*. Like unforgiveness, I would estimate that about 75% of the population has a root of it in their subconscious mind. Those that have the soul iniquity of jealousy assume that everyone has it and that just isn't the case. Jealousy is not like pride; not everyone has it in the subconscious mind. However, of the 75% of people that do carry it, there can be different amounts or stages of it in different people. One person may a grape-size black spot of jealousy that rarely manifests. While another person may have a grapefruit-sized ugly, diseased, cancerous tumor of jealousy that ruins relationships and causes the person to be consistently bitter and hostile.

Most people think that jealousy and envy are the same thing. Although the two words are synonymous, there are some slight differences. Envy is the presence of discontentment or ill will at another's good fortune or a dislike for a person who has what they want. Jealousy is a little more layered because there are different types of jealousy. The positive side of jealousy means to guard or protect something or someone. The negative side means either overprotective or envious. The negative side of jealousy is dangerous because a person's thinking can become distorted. Jealousy causes an evil passion to be stirred up in a person's imagination.

Jealousy/envy is an ugly sin, but our culture does not recognize the seriousness of this soul iniquity. In some circles, jealousy is considered a compliment. One woman may say to another, "Your husband is so great; I'm so jealous," or say, "I love your new furniture; I'm so envious." Most people in our culture don't recognize it as a bad thing because it is treated as a compliment.

When someone desires what someone else has, they are being short-sighted. They don't know the other person's whole story. They don't know the struggles they have faced or the challenges that they may have been through. Maybe that person endured endless hours of studying and training to educate themselves so they could afford that car you envy. Were you willing to pay the same price? If you were, there is still time. Improve yourself so you can make more money. Someone else may be jealous of a person's trim body. Well, are they willing to pay the price of dieting and exercise to get a trim body? Recognize that most of the things that people envy came at a price. What they achieved can be accomplished by others that are willing to pay the same price.

Some belongings and features that people may envy are not necessarily things that the person that has them, has earned. Perhaps fortune just smiled on them and blessed them. Maybe a woman just naturally has a pretty face. Well, good for her. Why does that have to affect you? You should be happy for her and not angry with her.

Jealousy has never been an issue for me. I am one of those in the 25% group who do not have jealous thoughts. But even if I did have a root of it, I think I would have been able to uproot it when I was an altar worker for a large church in the 90's. I talked to all kinds of people in the prayer room, and they shared personal information with me. I saw that the beautiful people still had problems. They had insecurities and plenty of life struggles. Their lives were not better; and they weren't happier. The same was true for those that had an abundance of money.

Their money didn't make them happy. It didn't bring them peace and certainly didn't resolve their relationship issues.

If a person made better choices than us and they were rewarded for it, good for them. Let them be a role model for us to make improvements in our own lives. Don't curse them or envy them. Everybody has struggles and just because we may think another person's problems pale in comparison to our own, doesn't make it true. We have no idea what their emotional or intellectual capacity is. They may not be able to handle our struggles and we may very well be stronger than they are emotionally. When we start comparing, we start playing God. We are telling God that He was unfair in His choices, and we deserved better. We are telling God that He made a mistake; He shouldn't have blessed the people we may be jealous of, and their blessing should have come to us.

Envy Breeds Evil

Envy is a breeding ground for evil. James 3:14-16 says, *"But if you have bitter envy and self-seeking in your hearts, do not boast and lie against the truth. This wisdom does not descend from above, but is earthly, sensual, demonic. For where envy and self-seeking exist, confusion and every evil thing are there."*

Contention, strife, and discord thrive when jealousy abounds. In fact, this may surprise you, but out of all the *diseases of the soul*, I consider jealousy to be the most dangerous one for a company, organization, or church. I have had employees with a strong root of jealousy and all they did was bring strife and division to the company. I can usually spot it a mile away. If there is a person that is always gossiping and bringing drama, nine times out of ten, it is because there is a root of jealousy in them. I have observed nasty cat fights between jealous women. Jealous people will usually try to pit others against the person they don't like. They will demean and discredit in subtle and overt ways. They are usually two-faced; they may be considerate to their face but revile them behind their back.

As well, people with jealousy can team up together and accomplish great evil. We can see examples of that in the Bible. Josephs brothers were jealous of him, so they sold him into slavery. The pharisees were jealous of Jesus, so they turned into a murderous mob demanding his death. When jealous people link arms with other jealous people, they tend to feed off each other's energy and a murderous mindset can grow. As a group, they will become more venomous than they would as an individual.

In today's world, a band of jealous people may not show up with pitch forks demanding a person's physical death, but they can certainly assassinate the character of someone. That murderous spirit can destroy a person's career, relationships, or reputation. People with a root of jealousy seem to be drawn to each other like magnets and when they are together, they can do great harm to any group dynamic.

Manifestations of Jealousy/Envy

Critical Remarks and Gestures

A very common manifestation of jealousy is critical comments and gestures. Jealous people usually put others down to make themselves look better. Their remarks tend to be subtle, and the person often thinks they are being funny when they do it. Most culprits don't realize that their verbal jabs are rooted in jealousy.

Years ago, I had a roommate that often criticized me but always said she was "just kidding" when she did it. One day, I confronted her about it, and she said I was overreacting. She said she saw how my sister Stephanie and I always played around with lighthearted bantering back and forth and she was just doing the same thing. In my roommate's mind, her verbal digs and criticisms were of the same caliber as what my sister and I did, but they weren't. My roommate's comments resonated with a murderous tone and were usually in a public setting. The comments were different than my sister's because they had a different spirit behind them. On the outside she would smile and laugh, but her subtle and innocent banter carried an ugly, angry undertone.

Jealous people often try to influence others to have the same views as them. They want a group of people to dislike the people they dislike. They will often express non-verbal criticisms by their vocal tone and inflections as well as the facial gestures and body language. It's their way of communicating, "I don't like this person, and neither should you."

Comparing Yourself

A person with a root of jealousy can't help but compare themselves to others. For them, it isn't a random thought that they may have every few months. For the jealous person, their mind just automatically compares themselves to others. Most of the time, they are not even aware they are doing it because they don't pay attention to their thoughts.

People with a stronghold of jealousy may not have a sense of self-worth or a true sense of their own identity. As a result, they use comparison to evaluate and validate themselves. They try to find their own identity in others, and in many cases, they hold other people up as benchmarks.

A woman with five sisters may constantly compare herself with her sisters. She may look at the one with the most challenges and setbacks and project those elements onto herself, or she may look at the most successful sister as her cap of what she can accomplish. She has no potential unless it's seen in others close to her. That woman may even be a hypochondriac. Her identity is based on comparison, so she may project the physical ailments and emotional challenges of her sisters onto herself.

People who carry jealousy may act as if they are full of confidence, but most of them don't have a real sense of identity. They don't understand their value to God. In their conscious mind, they believe God loves them but in their subconscious mind, they don't have that certainty. Many of them base their value on performance or appearance. Because they don't have a strong sense of identity, the opinions of other can easily affect them. A criticism can send their self-esteem into a downward spiral.

We must stop comparing ourselves. We must remember that each of us are *"fearfully and wonderfully made,"* (as it says in Psalms 139:14). God didn't mess up when He made us. All of us have attributes and flaws. When we envy something about someone else, we only look at a certain attribute and not the whole picture. We don't have all the pieces to the puzzle; we don't know what their life is really like or what they struggle with. We also don't know the price they might have paid to obtain some of the blessings they have.

Depression

Because jealous people are constantly comparing themselves with others, they can rehearse all the ways they don't measure up in their mind and that can open the door to discouragement and depression. They don't *"count their blessings,"* (as the Bible says in John 1:16), instead, they focus on what they don't have.

Demonic activity is common around jealous people. Demons will often whisper discouraging thoughts to a person that compares themselves. Remember, it's the devil's job to *"rob, steal, and destroy"* (as it says in John 10:10). The enemy of our soul will try to take advantage of any and all of our weaknesses. So, he will often try to bring added discouragement to a jealous person. Afterall, a jealous person has done half of the work for the demon. The person is already doing the comparing, the demon just needs to add fuel to the fire and whisper thoughts like "you will never have what they have," "you are worthless," and "give up, why do you even try?"

Copycat

Another common expression of jealousy (which can also be a clue that a person is jealous) is copycat behavior. Jealous people want what others have, and in order to get it, they copy them. They can copy their hairstyle, their clothing choices, their laugh, their walk, their speech pattern, or really anything about that other person.

In many ways, copycats are double minded. Because their identity is borrowed, it never seems to fit right, but they don't know why. After a while, they feel uncomfortable. So, they look for another change but don't know who to follow.

Diverts Attention

Carriers of jealousy hunger for attention so they can somehow receive their own self-worth. If attention is directed towards a person they don't like, they will attempt to divert the attention somewhere else. If their nemesis is getting complimented, the jealous person may try to change the subject or start talking about a different person. They will do anything to get the positive attention off of the person they don't like.

Distracts Attention

Not only will a jealous person try to divert attention away from a person they are jealous of, but they may also try to distract them, so they fail. For example, two college girls share a dorm room. The jealous student may see that the other one is trying to study so she may do things that distract her like play music too loud or talk on the phone. Or in a work situation, one employee may have a big presentation to make in a half hour, but a jealous co-worker may interrupt her with questions, so she doesn't have time to finish her presentation.

Easily Bugged

Jealous people are usually easily bugged by the people they carry jealousy towards. Minor annoyances, whether real or perceived, can become huge personality flaws in the mind of a jealous person. There have been several times that friends of mine, who carried jealousy, harshly criticized other people for comments or actions that weren't wrong. My jealous friends were surprised that most people weren't bothered by the people they didn't like. To them, the other person was a neon light of annoyance but, in reality, their comments and actions weren't a big deal. The offensive action was all in the imagination of the jealous person.

A jealous person often rationalizes that the things that bug them about a person, disqualifies that person. Years ago, I had a roommate that always complained about her supervisor. One time, she had overheard a conversation her supervisor had with her daughter. That conversation really bothered my roommate, so she quickly labeled the supervisor as a bad manager because she thought she was a bad mother. My roommate surmised in her mind that the woman didn't deserve to be a supervisor because she didn't have a good relationship with her daughter. The real issue was that my roommate was jealous of her supervisor's authority. She felt she could do a better job and she used the bad mother reasoning to justify her contempt towards her boss. First, hearing one call is not enough evidence to label a person as a bad parent. And second, just because she had an angry moment with her child on the phone, does not mean it would impact her performance as a supervisor.

Remember, jealousy distorts the reality of the carrier. In their mind, perceived annoyances and flaws of a person, disqualifies that person from their position. And unfortunately, a jealous person will try to convince other people that the person they are jealous of is unqualified or disqualified.

Strife

All of us have soul iniquities. It is part of living in a fallen world. However, as I mentioned earlier in this chapter, jealousy is one of the most dangerous character flaws to a group, company, or church. Strife and contention always follow when there is a jealousy problem.

Years ago, I met three women from a Bible-believing, Spirit-filled church in Los Angeles. The women asked me to pray for a new church building for their church. As I prayed for them, a word of knowledge came up in my spirit. I sensed that God wanted to bless that church, but He wouldn't until a jealousy issue was resolved. The Holy Spirit told me that the degree of jealousy was so potent in that church, that blessing them with a new building would harm them. As church members were blessed financially and gave to the church for the new building, the murderous mindset of jealousy would attack the blessed ones and would destroy the church and cause it to disband. The word of knowledge was for the church to address and purge jealousy before God would bless them financially.

Closing Thoughts

We don't have to look very hard to see the fruit of jealousy. We can see it on our jobs, in our church, among our friends, and maybe even in our home. When there is ugliness in the atmosphere, do a quick check to see if it may be based in a jealousy issue.

Check in with God to see if you are the one causing the strife and drama. If you are, take active measures to work on jealousy. If you don't, there is a good chance you can ruin relationships, careers, and even work against God plans.

Nine

Rebellion

There are generational brackets (age groups) that glorify rebellion. The baby-boomers that were teenagers in the 60's and 70's were encouraged to embrace rebellion with movies like, *Rebel Without a Cause* and songs like, *Born to Be Wild*. And now the Millennial and Gen Z generations have been persuaded to choose their own brief structure in a world where nothing is considered sinful except labeling something as sinful. They have embraced the notion that there is no absolute truth and that everyone should create their own version of truth. Well, right is right and wrong is wrong, regardless of the social mores of the day.

What is rebellion? It's an opposition to one in authority or an instance of defiance or resistance. Is all rebellion bad? No. We know that history records rebellions that have risen up to combat tyrannies and dictatorships. There are absolutely some rules, guidelines, and mandates that we should oppose if they lead to the removal of our God-given rights. But I am not talking about the type of rebellion that seeks to correct social injustices. I am talking about rebellion towards authority figures in our life. I'm talking about disobedience to the instructions given to us by our parents, our teachers, our employers, our government, and even God. Rebellion in the heart of a person tells them that they know better than the authority figure. There is something within a rebellious person that says "No, I'm going to do things my way."

Most of us rebel in little ways. I don't know very many people that always obey the designated speed limits. I don't know anyone that has always obeyed the instructions of their parents. We have within us a streak of stubbornness and independence that prompts us to be the captain of our own life. We don't want rules that we don't see as beneficial and useful. We have common sense. We know what is good. We know what is safe. We don't want some headmaster forcing us to do things their way.

As true as all that is, there must be order and structure; there must be guidelines, so people and organizations don't get harmed, bogged down, damaged, or chaotic. Parents instruct their children to keep them safe and ensure that they grow up to be successful and have good moral conduct. Schools have rules in place to manage education effectively in an impartial environment. Employers have specific protocols designed to increase productivity and efficiency. State and local governments have laws and statutes in place to ensure the safety and well-being of its citizens. We don't get to make our own rules and still be a functioning member of society.

Most of us conform to the expectations that society puts on us. Just because we have a little bit of stubbornness in us doesn't mean that we have a soul iniquity of rebellion. Having an independent nature in us is what enables an entrepreneur spirit and sparks our creativity to craft and develop new ideas and businesses.

Teenager Rebellion

Most (but not all) children go through a rebellious stage when they hit their teenage or preteen years. The degree of the rebellion can vary greatly between the children. One child can have very mild rebellious behavior that may involve delayed obedience and an eye roll every once and a while. While another child may turn into a ranging monster that cusses out their parents, steals, breaks things, and even runs away. The parents' behavior can influence the rebellion level in their child but, ultimately, it is determined by how the child processes their mental conclusions and emotions.

I wasn't a rebellious child. In fact, I don't remember any yelling or door slamming on my part. I was a good kid. I didn't misbehave until I turned 19 years old and at that point, I moved out of my parents' house. I was the youngest of seven children that grew up in the same house. Being the youngest, I witnessed the rebellion of my siblings. I saw what they got away with and what activities and attitudes got them in trouble. I had examples to go by, so I didn't make the same mistakes. My parents weren't as strict with me as they were with the older children. I was very involved in the youth group at church and the theater department at school. I acted mature and responsible, so they treated me that way.

Typically, teenage rebellion doesn't necessarily mean there is a root of rebellion in the child's subconscious mind. Teen rebellion is more about that child trying to gain independence and discover their own identity. Preteens and teenagers experiment to figure out their likes and their dislikes. They test themselves to see how they can handle more mature activities like staying up later and being home alone. Their school life and friendships often take on a more important role to them than their home life so it can seem like the child is shutting out the family. Teens can be a walking contradiction. They want their absolute freedom one minute; then they want the security and protection of their parents the next.

As of this writing, my daughter is 12 years old. Like most kids her age, she experiments with rebellious behavior as her way of demonstrating her maturity. When she says something that is a little defiant, I do address it with her. Some behaviors should be corrected early on before they get more engrained. My daughter (like most kids) needs to know she doesn't get to disrespect her mother even though she is in a season of self-discovery and increasing independence. She needs boundaries and guidelines but not in a "do as I say and not as I do" kind of way. Modeling certain behaviors is much better than just barking out rules. As well, explaining the reasons for parental decisions gives a child a much better understanding of the situation and helps them see the logic. The reason most kids break the rules is they don't agree with the rules and boundaries. Giving adolescents an understanding of the "whys" will help them make better choices.

Rebelling Against God

We have a natural desire within us to be the boss of our own lives and that is a good thing. However, if we have made Jesus the Lord of our lives, that means we have surrendered the leadership position to Him.

Most Christians display rebellion towards God in some area of their lives and they may be oblivious to the fact that it is rebellion. Even though God may be telling us to do something or stop doing something, we refuse to obey. We may not be consciously making a choice to rebel against God, but we continue to ignore His instructions. After continued disobedience, we can act as if we don't know what the problem is. We may wonder why the heavens are silent, why our prayers are not answered, and why God seems distant. In these cases, we are backslidden, and we may not even realize it. Disobedience is rebellion and will cause us to feel distant from God.

None of us live perfect lives and I am not talking about being perfect. I am talking about obeying specific things we know God has told us to do. We may know God told us to start a certain project, but we haven't started it yet. Or God told us not to date a certain person, but we like them, so we haven't broken off that relationship. Or we sensed God wanted us to register for a class, but we kept putting it off.

There are specific instructions that God gives us that He expects us to follow. Oftentimes, we won't understand the *whys* of God's instruction.

Years ago, in 2001 or 2002, I was scheduled to go with my friend Betty to a Christian conference in Ohio. The trip was planned, and my flight was booked. Then, I distinctly heard the Holy Spirit tell me not to go. I didn't know why. When I told Betty I wasn't going, she was mad at me. But I couldn't give her a reason except that God said not to go. I still don't know why I wasn't supposed to go. However, that experience reminds me to also try to get a "yes" from God before I book a flight.

One time in 2018, a friend and I were going to go to an event in San Diego. Neither one of us had our daughters that night, so we planned to go. She was excited about going all that day. I wasn't as excited, but I thought no harm could come from it. Then, about a half hour before we were supposed to leave, I sensed God telling me not to go. He didn't give a reason why. I didn't want to disappointment my friend, so I didn't tell her, and we started off on our journey.

As I was driving on a narrow highway with no streetlights in the hills of San Diego County, I almost got into a major car accident. I was in the middle lane of a 3-lane highway, and I had cars on both sides of me. Suddenly a metal chair flew off a truck and came bouncing towards my car. I tried to swerve a little to miss it, but I couldn't change lanes without hitting a car. The metal chair ended up hitting my car and we felt the impact of it. Thankfully, the car was still drive-able, but it did do some body damage.

Could that have been the reason why God told me not to go? Perhaps. Maybe He told me not to go because He knew the devil had something up his sleeve to harm me. I do believe angels protected us, so it was only a little body damage to my car and not something worse.

God often gives us instructions without telling us why. It isn't our job to understand the why. It's our job to just trust and obey.

Obedience to God is essential, not just the specific promptings for our individual lives but also obedience to Biblical commands. I shared the next story in another book, but I feel compelled to share it again.

I was driving on Jamboree Road in Tustin Ranch heading towards the foothills of Orange in Southern California around eight one evening. I saw a dog on the sidewalk about 50 feet in front of me. It looked like he had just jumped the block wall fence from his family home. I immediately started to slow down. The speed limit on the street was 45 mph, but most cars were going faster. I didn't see any people, so I was concerned for the dog's safety.

Sure enough, the dog, which looked to be a one-year-old boxer, started to run in the street. It snuck by the first two cars in the first two lanes but then got hit by the third car in the third lane. None of the drivers stopped or even slowed down, not even the car that hit him. It was insane. That part of Jamboree Road wasn't well lit; drivers were only paying attention to other car's break lights. They weren't looking out for animals, pedestrians, or bicycles.

By this time, I had pulled off to the side of the road. I had my two-year-old daughter in a car seat in the back and I had my three-year old cocker spaniel in the car. I thought for a second how I could open my door without my dog jumping out. In that split second, the dog in the street was hit by a second car. I was screaming at cars to stop but none of them heard me. I was panicking. As I had my hand on the handle to jump out, I stopped. Questions raced through my mind:

Would the cars even see me?
Would the cars hit me?
Is the dog still alive?
How heavy is he?
Can I lift him on my own?

When I looked up again, I saw the dog trying to crawl away, but he was hit by a third car. Then immediately after that, a fourth car hit him and killed him. It all happened so fast; yet it was slow motion to me.

I was devasted. That night, as I was trying to go to sleep, I couldn't get the images out of my mind. I asked God why He allowed me to witness such a horrible thing. I felt like there had to be a lesson in it and there was. As I thought about it, I knew the dog's owners would be extremely sad when they discovered what happened. They had provided a loving home for that new member of their family. However, the dog's curiosity got the best of him, and he decided to jump over the wall. He went outside the boundaries that his owners had given to him, and it was fatal. The dog jumped into traffic. It wasn't the owners' fault. The dog made two stupid mistakes: the first one was jumping over the wall and the second was attempting to run across the street.

I believe God provides supernational protection to His kids, but that protection comes when we obey His instructions. If we have developed our discernment to clearly hear the voice of the Holy Spirit, more protection is provided because we can hear God warning us more often about situations.

However, in a general sense, we have more protection when we stay within the boundaries that God has given us. We are more insulated from harm if we follow the moral guidelines that the Bible teaches. There are activities that invite the kingdom of darkness into our lives and steering clear of those areas will make it harder for the devil to steal, kill, and destroy in our lives.

There may be natural consequences for breaking man's laws and God's laws. If you rob a bank, there are consequences for your actions that will impact your life in a very negative way. If you cheat on your wife, don't expect your affair to stay a secret. There can be very damaging results from your actions. If you lie and cheat to get ahead, those lies can come back to bite you.

God's protection doesn't mean we are exempt from the repercussions of our own actions. God goes out of His way to protect us, but when we step outside of His boundaries, we will be subject to consequences. God will always forgive us if we are truly repentant, however, our actions may have long standing results. We can't expect protection if we are leaving the boundaries (our walled in backyard) He has established for us, and we jump into traffic. We must endeavor to obey God, both the boundary principals He gives us in the Bible and in the specific instructions for our individual lives.

Demonic Activity

Not only does rebellion and continued disobedience position us outside of God's protective umbrella, it can invite demonic activity into our lives. First Samuel 15:23 says, *"For rebellion is as the sin of witchcraft."* Rebellion makes us a target and it empowers demons to work their wiles in our lives.

When I was an altar worker a larger church in the 90's, a woman approached me and asked me to come to her house after service to pray a demon off of her. When I got to her house, she described to me how a demon moves around inside of her body and physically bites her. She showed me bite marks on her back, thighs, and knees. She said it was very painful when it happened, and her two small children heard her screams of pain.

She proceeded to tell me that the demon told her it had a right to be there because she was in disobedience to God. Apparently, God had been telling her to stop smoking for a while and that was an area of continued disobedience for her.

Of course, the demon didn't have a right to be there. She was a blood-bought child of God, but she did have an open door to the dark side because she had continued disobedience in her life. As I was praying for her, the Holy Spirit reminded me that continued disobedience is a manifestation of rebellion and rebellion invites demonic activity. We had the authority to kick the demon out because it's not about our righteousness, but rather about the victory Jesus won on the cross. However, if we continue in rebellion, it is ignorant to think that the demon wouldn't come back.

When we root out rebellion and other *diseases of the soul* that God may highlight to us, we will be able to tell the devil, "You've got nothing on me." It doesn't mean that we will be exempt from demonic attacks, but it does mean we will carry greater spiritual authority to combat the kingdom of darkness. When there is less of us and more of

Christ shining through us, we carry more authority in the spirit realm. Our Adamic nature iniquities can block and hamper the Holy Spirit's operation. But when we take active measures to root out our iniquities, we allow the Holy Spirit to flow through us in a greater degree.

Rebellion doesn't just invite the devil to mess with us, it also can cause us to be used by demonic forces. We can unknowingly start to operate in a form of witchcraft, and we can cooperate with demonic forces. We can actually be used as instruments to come against the plans and purposes of God. If rebellion is present in our life, don't be surprised when the devil tries to use us as his puppet.

The *Disease of the Soul* of Rebellion

Not everyone that has the sin of disobedience in their life necessarily has a *disease of the soul* of rebellion in their subconscious mind. In fact, if I had to estimate a percentage of Christians that have a soul iniquity of rebellion, I would calculate around 15% to 20% so it isn't a large number.

I believe the soul iniquity of rebellion can be a *generational curse* or it can be a byproduct of another *disease of the soul*. It can be a secondary infection caused from not correctly treating the original sickness. For example, if a sinus infection is not treated with antibiotics, it can develop into bronchitis, a sore throat, or an ear infection. Rebellion can be the same way. It can take root if we haven't appropriately treated our pride, unforgiveness, hatred, prejudice, lack of discipline, envy and so forth.

Earlier in the book, I mentioned that my brother Ken had a root of unforgiveness that grew into a stronghold of offense, which spread to a root rebellion. He held great contempt for our father, which mutated into a rebellion against other authority figures. His history is a good example of how rebellion can be a secondary infection that was caused from a different soul iniquity.

I have also witnessed how rebellion can be caused by a *generational curse*. A friend of mine who didn't know her biological father because he passed away when she was very young, appears to have received the rebellion soul iniquity as a *generational curse* from him. From what her mother had told her about her father, it was a safe assumption that he carried rebellion in him based on information known about him.

My friend carries a root of rebellion. While it isn't prevalent all the time and can lay dormant at times, it is still there. What is interesting is my friend has a different biological father than her siblings and her siblings don't have a root of rebellion in them. Of course, I don't know every detail of my friend's childhood so I couldn't say with all certainty that her rebellion originated from a *generational curse*, but I do know her very well.

As you have probably gleaned by now, I am a student of human behavior. I have a knack for discovering repeat behaviors patterns in the people I am around. I have spent a lot of time around my friend's young daughter, and I have observed how rebellion has manifested in her. Granted, all kids are rebellious. Children are constantly testing boundaries as they grow and mature. And as of this writing, my friend's daughter hasn't hit the preteen rebellious stage yet. For the last four years, I have observed rebellion in the child numerous times, which I know is also in her mother, and is believed to be in her biological father as well.

I first noticed the rebellion in the little girl four years ago. We were at a restaurant and her mother had gone to the restroom and left us at the table together. There was a balloon at our table. My friend's daughter was constantly handling the balloon and I could tell it was irritating an older couple at a nearby table. And to be honest, it was bugging me as well. I told her to stop touching the balloon. She looked at me and in a very slow, methodical way, she wrapped her hand around the string of the balloon and then gave me a snarky glare. I couldn't believe the open defiance. This was a five-year-old child, and she was making a statement that she would not comply. This wasn't an impulse control thing, or she really wanted to play with the balloon thing. It was a *you're not the boss of me* thing.

That was many years ago, but that defiant thing is still in her. She is a great kid and really does have some wonderful qualities in her. But I've noticed that she has almost an auto-response thing in her to rebel. If she is in my car and making a weird noise and I ask her to stop, she will always do it one more time before she stops. Unlike with the balloon grab that was very deliberate, I see an auto-response behavior pattern in her when she is told to stop doing something. I do believe my friend and her daughter both have a stronghold of rebellion that was passed down to them as a generational curse.

Manifestations of Rebellion

Procrastination

Delayed obedience can be rebellion. We see this displayed quite often in children. A parent may tell their child several times to turn off their electronics and brush their teeth. The child doesn't respect the authority of the parent, so they chose to ignore it.

In adults, procrastination is worse than blatantly refusing to do something because with procrastination we are lying to ourselves and others. We remove the sense of urgency when it comes to matters of obedience and we give ourselves permission to ignore the issue. When we say we are going to do something later, what we are really saying is we refuse to do it now.

None of us are perfect and God doesn't expect us to be. However, if there is an action that God wants us to take or a behavior He wants us to correct and we keep procrastinating, we are in rebellion.

Defying or Ignoring Authority

Most people with a root of rebellion don't openly defy authority but they may. Most of the time, they will just ignore the authority figure and act like that authority has no bearing on their life. Sometimes pride can get in there and convince them that they are smarted than the authority figure and that is why they shouldn't be obeyed. It can manifest by being too casual with a new supervisor at work and not showing respect for their position. It can be demonstrated by ignoring the requests of the ushers at church to sit in a certain section. Or if a supervisor tells their team to move to another room, it can be exhibited by walking slower than everyone else or doing another activity first before heading to the other room. There are all sorts of subtle ways to disrespect those in authority positions.

Breaking Rules

Breaking rules is similar to ignoring authority but instead of it being directed towards a specific person, it is against a company, school, or government. A person with a root of rebellion has a subconscious blueprint in them that says, "rules don't apply to me." They will often do a form of compliance but put their own spin on it, so it isn't exactly obedience.

Stealing

I am not suggesting that everyone that has a root of rebellion steals. But stealing can be a manifestation of rebellion. It is a form of the *break the rules* thing that is in them. And even if a person with a root of rebellion has stolen in their past, doesn't mean that they have continued that behavior. People with the *break the rules* blueprint in them are more likely to do little things that they don't really think is wrong, like taking home office supplies or sampling food at the grocery store.

When someone with a root of rebellion does steal, it really isn't about them wanting the item they took. It is about them being on a quest to see what they could away with. There is something in them that longs to *upset the apple cart.*

Power Struggles

Just like a root of jealousy can generate power struggles, so can rebellion. In fact, the two soul iniquities are often present together when a person is opposing a team leader or supervisor. The rebellion in them says, "You're not the boss of me," and the jealousy says, "I deserve it more."

People with a root of rebellion don't like anyone to be in positions over them. Depending on the size of the company or organization, they may honor senior management, but will usually have issues with supervisors and middle management.

If a rebellious person is friends with someone in management, they may say or do things that would cause employees to disrespect that manager. They are not consciously trying to harm their manager friend by sharing embarrassing stories and their personal information. They are doing it to elevate themselves so they can ride the coattails of respect. However, that usually isn't the end result. Rather than the rebellious person gaining respect, the manager usually loses respect. Employees that know too much personal information about their manager will typically treat them too casually and they may feel more comfortable criticizing them.

Critical Remarks and Gestures

Diseases of the soul reside in a person's subconscious mind, so a person is usually unaware of their true motives when they say or do disrespectful things. Like my friend's daughter, they often have an auto-response behavior that says, "you're not the boss of me." It can be demonstrated in humor, subtle demeaning comments, facial gestures, or inflections in their voice. There are all sorts of subtle and overt ways rebellion can be expressed through a person.

Closing Thoughts

We need make sure we walk in obedience to God's direction for our lives and live within the boundaries He has set for us. I encourage you to take time and reflect on the possibility that you may have a root of rebellion in your heart. Ask God to tell you or ask Him to remind you of memories that may offer clues to answer that question. Even if you don't have a root of rebellion in your subconscious mind, are there any areas of continued disobedience? If there are, recognize that as rebellion and repent. Ask God to help you with it. Making those adjustments will only bring good into your life. Surrender it to God and He will help you.

Ten

Religious Pride

Religious pride can be hidden to the naked eye. It usually shows up in two ways.

1) Religious pride can be demonstrated when a person feels or acts morally superior. They don't appear to have challenges with external sins or vices, but they may ignore sins of the heart like pride, jealousy, greed or unforgiveness. This Pharisee type Christian will typically preach damnation to those who engage in sex outside of marriage or who struggle with alcohol or drugs. They are quick to recite the law, but they fail to demonstrate God's love when doing it.

2) Religious pride can also be diagnosed when a person is discussing their "pet doctrines." A pet doctrine is an opinion about a Bible passage or Christian practices. Their strong opinions can be based out of their personal experiences, popular social views, their church's position on the issue, or their own private research. Pet doctrines are often topics that people can cherry-pick Bible verses to support their views. When people have religious pride, they view themselves as more knowledge-able about certain Biblical topics.

Religious Pride in the Church

Most churches carry religious pride but display it in various ways and in different degrees. They assume they have the market corner on truth. Conservative churches usually pride themselves in being balanced. Pharisee type churches think they are the only ones who *"rightly divide the word of God"* (as the Bible talks about in 2 Timothy 2:15.) Pentecostal churches pride themselves in understanding and using the gifts of the Spirit. Charismatic churches may assume they are the only ones who experience freedom and liberty in their worship.

Are we surprised by the disunity among Christian churches? Between the religious pride and jealousy – we are a house divided.

If a church believes drinking alcohol is wrong, they often embrace a holier-than-thou posture towards those who think it is okay to drink. A church that believes alcohol is acceptable may label non-drinking churches as legalistic. Pet doctrines within churches can range from how to dress in church, to women preaching, to music style, to how to deal with the sick, to how to take an offering, etc.

The biggest expression of religious pride within a church is believing their church is better than other churches. Most of the time, the inferences of it are very subtle, and it doesn't register on most people's radar. Usually, a pastor will avoid sounding too prideful by saying their church is better than other churches but there may be subtle comments made that imply it. If a pastor does say it from the pulpit, there may be degrees of truth in their statement. However, the caution is to guard against religious pride.

Most pastors want their congregation to have loyalty to their church and the beliefs expressed by the church. Pastors recognize that they are responsible for their congregation, so they rationalize that they have to protect their flock from wrong doctrine. While it is true that pastors try to protect their people, many pastors use that as an excuse to invoke fear towards other churches. They want their congregation to fear other churches, so their people won't be led astray by wrong doctrines or so they won't lose church members to other churches. Whether it is boldly declared or simply implied, fear of other churches and denominations is infused into believers from the pulpit. The fruit of planting fear and glorifying your home church is religious pride. It breeds the thinking that says, "God is with us and not with you" and "we are right, and you are wrong."

The Pride in Religious Pride

If there was one thing that was made clear in the chapter on pride is that pride leads to deceptive thinking. Well, that is true with religious pride as well. The Pharisees in Jesus' day really believed that they were right, and Jesus was wrong. It was quite ironic. They prided themselves for their spiritual insights but instead, they had spiritual blindness.

Pride is deceptive in all its forms. Pride leads a person to believe that they know the truth when others don't. If there happens to be areas of ignorance, they don't view it as ignorance. Instead, they view those insights and teachings as wrong, wicked, unbalanced, or even heretical. And because pride hardens the ice layer between the conscious mind and the subconscious mind, even if revelational information was given to them, they would reject it. It wouldn't resonate as truth to them because their discernment is limited or blocked by their pride.

Manifestations of Religious Pride

Unteachable

We, as Christians, both individually and corporately, need to come to terms with the fact that we don't have it all figured out. Many of us have been taught the meaning of certain scriptures from our Sunday School teacher, or from a Bible school, but we have stopped learning right there. We have compartmentalized certain passages to mean certain things. We think that we understand the definition or interpretation, so we close the door to any more revelations. We fail to remember that the word of God is living and powerful and God can reveal new truths in scriptures we have read a hundred times. We subconsciously believe we have it all figure out, so we plug our spiritual ears when the Holy Spirit is trying to reveal new insights through the word of God.

Years ago, in the late 90's, I had the privilege of meeting a wonderful and kind pastor at a TBN seminar. It was a divine appointment. Several of those attending the seminar, including the pastor and me, spent several hours together in prayer and fellowship. To meet this man, you would think he was the most humble person on the planet.

Outwardly, he projected a spirit of humility, but he had an unteachable spirit. Because he carried the title of pastor, he viewed everyone in the group as spiritual children. While in the middle of pie and coffee at a local restaurant, I shared the concept of *diseases of the soul*. One person in our group was absolutely enthralled by what I was teaching but the pastor just shut me out. I could see it on his face. When I began to disclose what God has shown me, his countenance changed. What I was communicating was slightly different than how he defined the soul, so he automatically and unconsciously rejected it. Who was I to instruct him? Afterall, I was just a 35-year-old woman who sold real estate. What could I possibly know about the soul?

Proverbs 19:27 says, *"Cease listening to instruction, my son, and you will stray from the words of knowledge."* We need to guard our heart against having an unteachable spirit. Don't make assumptions about people. God can use a donkey to instruct us. We need to remain sensitive to the Holy Spirit regardless of the vessel God chooses to use.

This pastor was experiencing a very difficult season in his life and ministry. I believe God wanted to show him some things through me. I use this pastor as an example, but he isn't very different than most of us. We can cry out to God to give us direction, yet we may plug our ears when He tries.

Holier-than-thou Attitude

Why do we place degrees on sin? Why do we look down on people who drink or smoke, but we ignore our gluttony? Why do we shoot dirty looks at that brazen hussy who flirts with all the men, yet ignore our gossip?

Human nature has a tendency to scorn others who still struggle with issues that are not weaknesses for us. A thin person can look at an overweight person and think they aren't very spiritual because they can't get their flesh under control. A pompous pillar in the church may belittle a young man who struggles with lust. A seasoned pastor may discount the views of a young couple just entering the ministry because they haven't been around the block yet.

We need to check ourselves. Is there someone we hold in low regard because they struggle with a particular sin? We may be carrying spiritual pride. Are there friends or family members who we feel are spiritually inferior to us? We may be projecting a holier-than-thou attitude and may not even be aware of it.

One thing I want to make clear in addressing a holier-than-thou attitude is we need to be careful not to label others with it haphazardly. Oftentimes, the Holy Spirit will use other people to point out an area of sin in our life. If we feel convicted about our sin, we may lash out at the person who pointed it out to us and accuse them of acting holier-than-thou.

When I first started attending church again in May of 1994 (before I rededicated my life back to God), my sister Cindy confronted me about sleeping with my boyfriend at the time. I became very irritated at her and I accused her of acting holier-than-thou – meaning she was acting spiritually superior. I had lived in the world long enough to know my conscience was seared. In looking back on that situation later, I saw that my sister wasn't acting morally superior; she was trying to obey what she felt the Holy Spirit told her to do.

"Heavy Revvy"

I don't see this manifestation very often anymore, but I saw it a lot among the students at the two Bible colleges I attended. As a student would awaken to the hidden gems in the Bible, they would get excited and would share those revelations with anyone that would listen. There was nothing wrong with that. Students are allowed to be excited about the scriptures. However, there were times when some of the students embraced spiritual pride and were actually showing off their new discovery. The motivation behind sharing it was to try to elevate themselves rather than bless others. We always need to remain humble regardless of how special we may feel when God speaks to us through a scripture.

Wrong Conclusions

I was out to dinner one time with a well-known Christian leader and a music director. The three of us were having a perfectly nice dinner with the objective of the Christian leader getting to know the music director and vice versa. Halfway through dinner, the music director asked us a random question in a bit of a forceful tone. Before we could even understand the context of initial question, the music director started quoting random scriptures and then tried to make a conclusion. When I tried to stop him or at least slow him down to review the Bible verse he had just quoted, he quickly jumped around and quoted more verses. This happened a few times. The pastor and I had a hard time grasping what the man was even talking about or the points that he was trying to make. And somehow, when he saw the look of confusion on our faces, he took that as a note of victory like he proved his points. What was confusion on our faces, he probably assumed was marvel at his profound knowledge.

Apparently, after talking to a mutual friend a few days later, this theory explosion rant was a habit of his that he liked to spring on pastors. He would perform a scripture pinball game, and when the listeners couldn't keep up with the points he was trying to make, he would assume he validated his random, insignificant Biblical theories. That mutual friend said that most of the people that the music director had sprung that on hadn't even tried to understand or debate the claims he was making.

I have witnessed people taking scriptures out of context to form their own theories before but never like this. He had it down to an art form. It seemed like it fed his spiritual ego to debate pastors with his pointless revelations. His religious pride felt validated to quote scriptures that most pastors wouldn't have memorized. But from my perspective, he was doing fuzzy math. He was metaphorically saying "2+2 = 22." He was combining scriptures and twisting them to validate obscure and insignificant theories. He believed 2+2 = 22 rather than 2+2=4. Most people did not to challenge him because they couldn't break into his memorized speech.

The word of God is living and powerful, as it says in Hebrews 4:12, and I believe God has numerous revelations to share with the body of Christ that we haven't discovered yet. But this man's rant about the Apostle Paul had no bearing on anything relevant. To me, it seemed like the music director was trying to prove how spiritually knowledgeable he was. I was surprised by the music director that night. I had known him as an acquaintance for several years and I have known him to be kind, humble, and generous. And he is all those things, but he also has root of religious pride that I witnessed that night.

Isolation

Some people with religious pride isolate themselves and don't go to church. They embrace a belief that church isn't beneficial for them because they are more knowledgeable and spiritually mature than the pastor. They rationalize to themselves that they can do their own Bible study at home by themselves.

It may be true that they don't benefit very much from church. But the reason for that has nothing to do with the pastor's spiritual maturity. The reason a religiously prideful person doesn't benefit from church is their pride blocks their ability to receive. Their pride has caused their heart to grow cold, so it is more difficult for the Holy Spirit to communicate with them. Without authentic communication with the Holy Spirit, isolation can accommodate the person's imagination to embrace incorrect doctrines and wrong mindsets.

Critical

Being critical is probably the most common manifestation of religious pride. People with the soul iniquity of religious pride will often critique the pastor or his sermon as soon as they exit the church. Their mind searches for any and all perceived flaws. If the pastor made three points in their message, the prideful person may think of a fourth point that should have been made. Or they may challenge and disagree with something the pastor said. It is not uncommon for a religious person to belittle the pastoral staff with comments of perceived spiritual immaturity or carnality.

Religious people often think that other people have the same critical thoughts that they have. I have been around religious people that were shocked to find out that I didn't share their same critical views.

Religious people are usually quick to criticize other denominations and well-known pastors. They may label them as carnal, un-balanced, unscriptural, heretical, or just plain evil. Some religious people actually believe it is their job to inform others of the evils of ministries that are different from their own. They believe they are doing God's work by bashing preachers.

Closing Thoughts

Jesus denounced the Pharisees in His day, yet the Pharisees of today don't even know they are Pharisees. Religious people criticize pastors without any consideration that they are opposing God's chosen leaders. We need to be very careful not to be critical. We also need to test our hearts. Can our heart be hard? Are we unteachable? Have we formed contempt in our heart towards people who struggle with sins that are not weaknesses for us? We need to seek God and ask Him to show us if we have religious pride lurking in a hook and cranny of our heart.

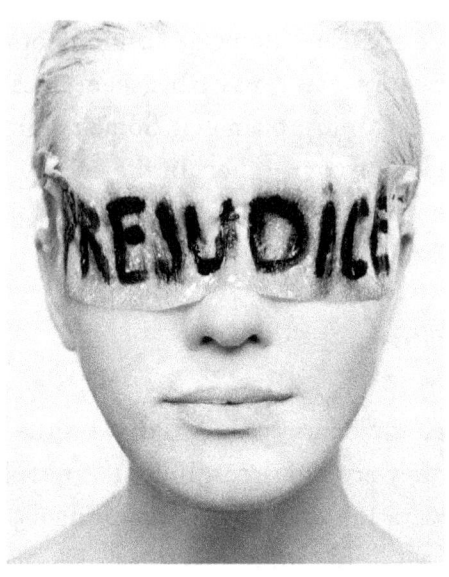

Eleven

Prejudice/Hatred

Prejudice is a preconceived bias towards a classification of people. That grouping of people can be based on race, ethnicity, religion, age, appearance, background, socio-economic status, interests, etc. Any group of people that interacts or identifies with others with similar backgrounds, preferences, or interests can become a target for hatred and discrimination. A prejudice person will fear, dislike, or devalue another person solely based on how they have categorized them. Their negative opinion will be formed before they know anything about the person they are judging.

Generally speaking, with racial prejudice, a person's age and where they grew up has a bearing on whether or not they may be bigoted. For example, a person that is 80 years old is more likely to have prejudice than someone who is 30 years old. Sixty years ago, discrimination was prevalent and socially acceptable. However, the tide started to turn in the 60's and 70's, and by the 80's; it was no longer appropriate to say and do things that would devalue or discredit people based on their skin color. And as you would suspect, people that grew up in the 80's typically didn't hear or see as much bigotry, so they were far less likely to embrace those wrong attitudes.

However, while parents may not have purposely taught their children to be prejudice, the children could have picked up on it in subtle ways. If a girl observed her mother crossing to the other side of the street because she feared a person walking towards her on the sidewalk, the child could adopt that fear without the mother saying anything. Or a son may see a simple expression on his father's face as he looked at someone with darker skin in a store and that facial expression may have sent a message to the son that he carried with him the rest of his life. Prejudice can be learned by nonchalant comments, expressions, and vocal tones. A parent may not sit their child down and tell them to fear other nationalities, but that message can be communicated.

Prejudice still exists today but to assume that all white people are racist is very wrong. Many of us have heard people, organizations, and some media outlets try to bring division by race-baiting to create strife and division. It's as if there is an agenda to promote prejudice so conflicts would occur.

Prejudice is a soul iniquity, and the simple truth is, not everyone has a stronghold of it in their subconscious mind. Much of the racial bigotry that used to exist has dissolved over the last 50 years.

Racial division isn't just Caucasians thinking less of African Americans. People of color often carry enmity against Caucasians. They too, have been taught to fear, distrust, and dislike a race based on their color. So racial dislike and distrust can be on both sides of the fence. A parent or grandparent may have experienced terrible racism in their childhood, so when they gave their child or grandchild advice, they may have imparted fear and distrust of white people in them.

Racism is usually cultivated in childhood, but it can arise in adults, as well. I was very surprised to discover that a man that I have known for 15 years has a stronghold of prejudice against Asian people. He used to complain about his two supervisors at his old job who were Vietnamese. I knew he didn't like them, but it surprised me that he allowed that disdain for them spread to other people and other nationalities. When my friend was looking to buy a used car from a private individual, he passed on a great deal simply because the seller was a Chinese man. I questioned him about it and told him his behavior was blatantly racist. He didn't deny it. His only defense was, he didn't trust him or any Asian people.

Who we associate with can also imbed bigotry in us. A gangbanger from east Los Angeles may be trained by his gang to hate cops. Before joining the gang, he may have been indifferent but after the gang's programming, he adopted the *group think* of the gang. If an ignorant, 18-year-old, white kid ended up in prison, he would probably get ingrafted into the white supremacy faction at the prison. He would be taught to hate all races except Caucasians. A LGBTQ group may indoctrinate a new member of their group to hate all born-again Christians by telling them that all Christians hate them. Biases and bigotries can be developed in all sorts of ways and not just by a person's parents.

The Bible tells us that prejudice is wrong. James 2:1-4 says, *"My brethren, do not hold the faith of our Lord Jesus Christ, the Lord of glory, with partiality. For if there should come into your assembly a man with gold rings, in fine apparel, and there should also come in a poor man in filthy clothes, and you pay attention to the one wearing the fine clothes and say to him, You sit here in a good place,"* and say to the poor man, *"You stand there,"* or, *"Sit here at my footstool,"* have you not shown partiality among yourselves, and become judges with evil thoughts?"* The Bible clearly tells us to not show partiality, not to prefer one people group over another. James 2:8-10 says, *"If you really fulfill the royal law according to the scriptures, "You shall* *love your neighbor as yourself," you do well; but if you show partiality, you commit sin, and are convicted by the law as transgressors. For whoever shall keep the whole law and yet stumble in one point, he is guilty of all."*

Throughout history, prejudices have existed. In Jesus' day, the Samaritans were discriminated against. In the dark ages, wars were fought over religion and people were hated for their beliefs. In some cultures, there was discrimination against redheads. In the 14th century, redheads were deemed to be untrustworthy friends, and in the 16th and 17th centuries, having red hair was a mark of being a witch. Historically Iranians are prejudice towards the Kurds. They treat Kurds like second class citizens and labeled as foolish. Kurds are used in jokes the same way Americans had Polish jokes in the 70's. Societies have labeled other cultures as foolish, evil, or untrustworthy and it's all ridiculous. The kingdom of darkness has used prejudice to spread division, strife, and hatred.

Everyone is different. While people of a certain nationality may have some similarities; individuals are different. Everyone has unique personalities with different character strengths and weaknesses. We must stop stereotyping people because when we do, we are judging them unfairly.

Types of Prejudice

Racial or Cultural

It has been my observation that bigotry manifests more when a person is uninhibited or stressed. Racism is one of those soul iniquities that can lay dormant for long periods of time but then pops up when a person is afraid, overwhelmed, or drunk.

Years ago, in the early 90's, I worked with a lady who grew up in the deep south and her family was wealthy. I was out to dinner with four of the women from work one evening, and the southern lady got drunk. Apparently, when she drank too much, her bigotry manifested. She was normally a very sweet and kind person, but something happened when she drank and became uninhibited. There was an Asian man in the restaurant and all the sudden she started verbally assaulting him because of his race. I was embarrassed to be sitting at the same table as her and we couldn't shut her up. She said the ugliest things to that poor man for absolutely no reason. He did nothing wrong. The next day at work when we confronted her about her actions, she shrugged her shoulders and said something about being like her mother and then she just laughed it off.

I think it is interesting that people can carry hostility for other races for years and it can go virtually undetected until something happens and it suddenly manifests. In the U.S., bias against middle easterners exploded right after 9/11. Hatred and suspicion were rampant back then, to the point that the average, law abiding citizens that happened to have a middle eastern background, were afraid to leave their house.

I have witnessed partiality in employment situations. I have seen managers prefer Caucasian candidates over those of color for no good reason. I have seen the reverse happen as well. I have seen black managers prefer black employees over others. I have seen the same with Hispanic and Asian managers, where they have hired people of their own ethnicity rather than base the hiring solely on the qualifications of the individuals. There shouldn't be two sets of rule books. The job should be offered to the most qualified individual, without partiality towards a specific ethnicity.

Political

Political prejudice has skyrocketed in the last ten years. Without going into detail, an executive order was signed on January 2, 2013 that basically nullified two acts that removed the penalties that media sources would face for purposely disseminating false information. As a result, news hasn't really been news since 2013. Instead, propaganda, political spin, embellishment, and fabricated stories have been labeled as news. Media companies push the narratives of their management, and it adds fuel to the fire creating a larger political polarization and intolerance among the American people.

The popularity of social media also helped create animosity and spread political contempt. Humorous political memes and false news articles created enemies from those that were once friends. The messaging said that all republicans were racists, and all democrats were socialist snowflakes. We know that isn't true, but we need to be aware of these false labels and make every effort to ensure we don't stereotype people just because they lean a certain way politically.

Appearance

People discriminate based on looks all the time. As much as we don't want to admit it, attractive people usually receive better service than unattractive people. I have witnessed it firsthand. In certain seasons of my life, when I have looked really bad, I have been overlooked while the clerk helped someone else. And in the times when I have looked good, I have watched as clerks went out of their way to help me while they overlooked other customers that had been waiting longer than me.

People make judgements about people based on their weight, their apparent wealth, and their beauty. We stereotype, categorized, and make value judgements based on appearance even though it shouldn't be that way.

Age

Years ago, in my late 20's, I was the youngest female manager at a Fortune 500 computer manufacturer. I encounter age discrimination. I received different reactions when I met clients face to face with whom I had built a relationship with over the phone. All of them had thought I was older, and they were surprised to find out I was still in my 20's. Some of them respected me more, thinking I must be an overachiever, while others had a negative reaction. They seemed to discount me and their respect level towards me declined.

Age discrimination is a pretty common occurrence in the business world. Most companies want employees in a certain age bracket. It depends on the industry, of course, but some companies are very discriminatory based on age. They have a concern that employees that are young will be too flakey and ignorant. And they fear older employees may be too set in their ways or have health issues which could hamper their performance.

Gender

I have experienced some gender discrimination as well in my life. There was discrimination at the computer manufacturer I worked at in the late 80's and early 90's. In fact, one time I was on the phone with a New York computer shop owner, and he said, "Listen honey, let me talk to your boss."

I responded back by saying, "My name is not Honey, and I am the boss of this division. If you want this equipment, you deal with me." That wealthy, rude, New York businessman's initial gender bias assumed I was just a secretary and that I wasn't the head of that division. He and I ended up doing several transactions together and actually became friends while I worked there. On one business trip to New York, he rolled out the red carpet for me. He took me out to an expensive dinner and even let me use his limo and driver to meet up with my other customers while I was in New York.

The real estate industry doesn't have a history of gender discrimination or bias. However, every once in a while, I would stumble upon it. Remember that nice, older preacher that I met at the TBN seminar, the one whose religious pride manifested as an unteachable spirit? Well, in our lengthy discussion, he mentioned that he used to sell real estate. He cautioned me not to "turn hard" and to "keep my femininity." He recounted a couple of times that he had dealt with "hard, aggressive women" in real estate transactions that had a "hard edge to them and didn't act like ladies."

It sounded to me like it hurt his male ego that he got beat by women in some real estate transactions. Gender doesn't come into play when you have a fiduciary responsibility to act in the best interest of your client. The preacher did have gender bias if he expected female real estate agents to roll over and allow male agents to get the upper hand just because they were male.

While the gender discrimination has diminished over time, it is still prevalent in some industries and businesses. There are some jobs that are better suited for men that require more physical strength. However, for the most part, the majority of occupations are well suited for both genders.

Manifestations of Prejudice and Discrimination

Critical

A high percentage of people with prejudice are unaware they have it. They don't know that their motive for being critical of someone could be because of a subconscious iniquity. A bigoted person who criticizes those they hold biases against, will usually believe their criticisms are justified. Sometimes, the criticisms can be so subtle the person won't even realize they are being critical. They believe they are making truthful statements.

Suspicious

Prejudices can be expressed through suspicion. Because the carriers of prejudice often have an unfounded fear of a certain category of people, their thoughts and behaviors will have an undertone of suspicion. It may mean projecting a mistrust onto the person and assuming they aren't being totally honest with you.

The suspicion may not necessarily be targeted at the person directly. It can be directed to a peripheral detail. For example, in a real estate transaction where the seller knows the potential buyers are African American, they may question the validity of the buyer's prequalification letter more than they would if the buyers were Caucasian. They may *"err on the side of caution"* by asking for additional documentation when discussing a financial transaction.

Ignore or Avoid

A person with prejudice may not make any derogatory comments at all. Instead, they may just overlook the person and be more impressed with another candidate. In hiring situations, they may be overly excited about a detail of a person's resume that they are not prejudice against. Or in a real estate transaction where there are multiple offers on a home, the sellers could just have a good feeling about another party. They don't criticize the minority buyers, but they just prefer another couple. They may even fool themselves into believing that it just feels right in their gut to go with a certain party.

Easily Bugged

Carriers of prejudice can be easily bugged, and they may not even know why. They can get angry or irritated and be totally unaware that the root of it is bigotry. When hatred and prejudice are present, strife will abound. Proverbs 10:12 says, *"Hatred stirs up strife, but loves covers all sins."*

I had a friend years ago who was half Mexican. She disliked the fact she was half Mexican, so when people asked her about her lineage, she would overemphasize the ethnicities in her that were more Caucasian. She associated her Hispanic heritage with poverty, pregnancy, and gangs. As a result, she became bigoted against all Mexicans. When she met or interacted with Mexican people, she became hostile and everything they said or did bugged her.

Defensive

Another common manifestation of bigotry of defensiveness. A person who struggles with prejudice often battles the issue in their mind. Their behavior can almost seem defensive because they can make too big of an argument in the other direction. Years ago, I heard a preacher that pontificated with passion for 20 minutes that African Americans and Caucasians were equal. I don't think there was anyone in the audience that didn't agree with that. He went on and on and it made me wonder if he was trying to convince himself. His overly defensive stance made me think bigotry was an issue for him.

Closing Thoughts

Prejudices are not as prevalent in the United States as they used to be, but they still exist. I encourage you to seek God and ask Him if you harbor prejudice, fear, or aggression towards a certain group of people. If you do, recognize it for what it is, repent, and ask God to help you identify thoughts and actions that reflect that pet sin.

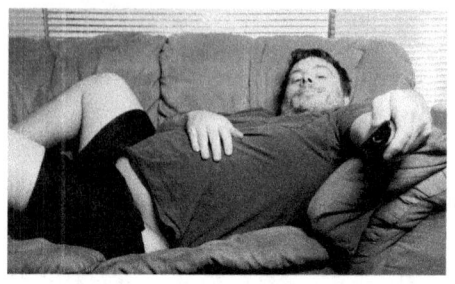

Twelve

Weak Willpower

You may wonder: How can weak willpower be a *disease of the soul?* Is letting our carnal, fleshly nature rule us really an iniquity? Well, it certainly can be. Self-control is about more than how often we exercise. It involves overcoming addictions, controlling what we say, managing our bodies, our time, and our money. We need to control our fleshly desires for food, comfort, laziness, and pleasure. That doesn't mean that we never eat a donut. But it does mean we shouldn't eat two or three of them a day. It means we control our flesh nature, and our flesh nature doesn't control us. Whatever the area is, we have the power to control ourselves and not be a slave to our carnal nature.

If you have read the first paragraph of this chapter, then congratulations, self-discipline is something most people don't want to talk about, read about, or think about. The mere mention of it can be a source of conviction and/or condemnation for many people. When reading this chapter, remember that God's love for us is not based on our works. He is head-over-heels in love with us regardless of how strong our discipline level is. However, our works are important because they will determine whether or not we are successful in life.

We know our soul is not instantly zapped renewed and perfect when we surrender our life to God. Not all of our bad habits miraculously disappear overnight. We probably will still have areas of our life that we will need to work on. We understand that it is our job to renew our mind to will of God which includes uprooting sinful and self-sabotaging behaviors.

How we view ourselves (our identity) can influence whether we are successful or not when we make self-discipline decisions. Our identity is housed in our subconscious mind, so a majority of our discipline issues are rooted in our identity. For example, if we think we are fat, we will stay fat. Our identity will sabotage our weight loss efforts so our circumstances (and outward body) lines up with what we believe about ourselves.

Our dreams can often tell us how we view ourselves. Does a person who is trying to quit smoking see themselves as a smoker in their dreams? If so, being a smoker is part of their identity so it may be a little harder to quit. Years ago, after I surrendered by life to God in 1994, I had a dream, and I was smoking in the dream. I remember thinking at the time how strange it was that I was smoking in my dream when I hadn't smoked for six months. I thought it was interesting that my subconscious view of myself was out of sync with my reality. Dreams can show us ourselves and they can even help change our identity. With these discipline areas, ask God to help you. Ask God to give you dreams that line up with the future He has for you.

None of us are perfect, so does that mean that everyone has a soul iniquity of weak willpower? No. Just because most people have areas of their life where they lack self-discipline, doesn't mean that area is a soul iniquity. To put it in gardening terms, let's equate these self-control areas as weeds. Most of us have weeds in our front garden. We know we should be more diligent to remove the weeds, but we are busy, and the weeds are not our priority. Weeds are an annoyance, and they can spring up out of nowhere. However, weeds are relatively easy to pull out; you don't need a tractor to uproot them. You, as an individual, can pull them up. However, there are people that don't just have a few little 5-inch-tall weeds; they have weeds that have grown into 5-foot-tall stalks that can't be easily uprooted. The stalks are thick and sturdy, and the person can't pull them out of the ground because the root system is too strong. Those weeds that are 5 feet tall are the strongholds in own life.

People with those kinds of self-discipline strongholds need help. If the issue is obesity, they may turn to weight loss surgery. If the issue is drugs or alcohol, they may seek help from AA, Celebrate Recovery, or even a rehab treatment. The key to diagnosing if a self-discipline area is a soul iniquity or not is, can the person correct it on their own? Has the person tired and failed enough times to admit that it is a stronghold?

In the *Diseases of the Soul* chapter, it was mentioned that the twelve soul iniquities are usually embedded in us because of: 1) *a generational curse*, 2) an event or incident from our past, or 3) a demonic attachment. If we look at some areas of self-discipline, it's easy to see how they can originate from one of the three of these.

1) A Generational Curse. If a man is a womanizer like his father was before him, people may say, "The apple doesn't fall far from the tree." This statement implies that the son has the same sex addiction or adulterous nature that his father had or has because it's a *generational curse*. An iniquity that is not dealt with or repented of can get passed down through DNA to a person's children.

2) An Event from Our Past. Some areas of weak willpower can be caused from events or memories from our past. It doesn't have to be a specific traumatic event; it can just be caused by what may have been modeled to us. If a child watched their parents overeat and glorify food as a reward, they will most likely do the same. It is their normal. It was how they were raised. So, while the person may have a desire to be thin, they will ultimately follow their identity of who they think they

are supposed to be. If a person grew up with a messy bedroom, they will most likely have more challenges keeping a clean home as an adult. It can be done. But it is a habit that will need to be broken and may not come easily for some people.

3) A Demon. A *disease of the soul* can certainly have a demon at its root. I used to know a woman that I believe had a gambling demon. She mortgaged her house to pay off gambling debt but then spent that money gambling and never paid the gambling debt. I know because I was the loan officer for her refinance, and I saw her financial records. Gambling ruined her life. It wasn't a fun hobby for her. It was a compulsion. It was an addiction. Some addictions have a demon at their core that drives, pushes, and compels people into vices.

The Disruptors

There are three different types of sabotaging forces that can come against us when we set out to change a behavior pattern. So, while we struggle with our own willpower, we may have to also contend with one or all three of these additional sabotaging influences.

1) Comfort Zones. The first disrupting force is one that I have mentioned before and that is our comfort zones. We all have borders and boundaries built into our subconscious mind that flags our internal sabotaging forces when we start to cross a line into the unfamiliar. Those internal restrictions can pertain to our weight, our income, our relationship status, or any number of things. Those internal limitations may be earmarked very differently than what our desires are.

I have a tall friend that I have known for 20 years. Since I have known her, her weight has fluctuated been between 210 lbs. and 275 lbs. She has weighed 210 lbs. a couple of times but never under it. A year and a half ago, she had weight loss surgery. After her surgery, she got down to 210 lbs. and she currently vacillates between 210 and 225 lbs. Why did she stop losing weight at 210 lbs.? She would look great at 180 lbs. She stopped at 210 lbs. because that was the lowest weight in her comfort zone. If she tried to push lower than 210 lbs., her body, her flesh nature, would fight her with self-sabotaging behavior. I would dare to venture that she won't dip below 210 lbs. until she is able to get a new picture of herself at a lower weight branded into her subconscious mind. For her, the key to weighing under 210 lbs., would be to correct her internal boarders (comfort zones) she has established in her subconscious mind.

There is nothing unique about my friend with the 210 lbs. plateau. Most of us have weight ranges embedded into our subconscious mind. Look at young women who get pregnant while they are thin. The majority of them bounce back to their pre-baby weight soon after they give birth. Why? Do they have special bodies with special metabolisms? Usually not. The reason most of them go back to their pre-baby weight right away is, their internal comfort zone drives their weight loss. They don't feel like themselves at the heavier weights and that discomfort pushes them to lose their baby weight. Of course, not all thin people stay thin after having a baby. Some of them have more flexible internal boundaries so their comfort zone makes adjustments to accommodate the higher weight.

2) Psychological Fear or Disdain. Another disrupting force when someone is trying to show self-discipline can be caused by fear or disdain. (Since I used weight loss in the above sabotaging viewpoint, I will use it for this one as well.) I have known several women that have subconsciously sabotaged their weight loss because of psychological fears and even disdain. Women that were sexually abused have subconsciously packed on the pounds to try to make themselves less desirable. Their fear of being attractive to the wrong kind of men, has kept them fat. As a result, several of them have remained single. They want a relationship with a good man; however, they have built both an emotional wall around heart and a physical wall of extra weight around their body. I have known a couple of other women who secretly had

unforgiveness towards their husbands. Without intentionally doing it, they made themselves less physically attractive so they wouldn't be pressured to be physically intimate.

3) Demonic Forces. The third type of sabotaging force is demonic suggestion. The average person is clueless how much the spirit world influences our lives. Think back to that metaphorical angel on one shoulder and devil on the other. That analogy is truer than people realize.

There is a spiritual battle going on around us all the time. The kingdom of darkness knows that if they can get us to feel bad about ourselves, we won't walk in confidence and victory. So, of course, the devil will attack our self-esteem. He wants to us fail because if we succeed, it builds momentum in us. That victory and renewed hope, coupled with obedience to the Holy Spirit, can cause damage to the kingdom of darkness. It may sound a little narcissistic to consider that demons care what we weigh. Well, it isn't that they care, but that they know we care. They know if they can position us into discouragement or complacency, then they have won half the battle. That is why they will target us with temptation and discouragement, to stop our forward movement.

If the little imps can't get us with temptation, they may even try to slap us with a headache, knee injury, or back pain to stop us from exercising. And of course, the little imp demon assigned to us may try to get us feeling overwhelmed by causing problems in our life, so we don't have time to focus on our health.

The devil doesn't want us to succeed. He knows that if he can sabotage our success, it will affect our self-esteem and we won't be as effective for the kingdom of God. How many times have we stopped ourselves from stepping out in obedience to God because we felt disappointed in ourselves? Well, that's the goal of the dark side.

Types of Discipline Issues

Exercise

Most of us would admit that we should exercise more. We know doctors always tell their patients to exercise for a half hour, at least three times a week. Well, sometimes the Holy Spirit will tell us to follow our doctor's advice on exercise.

Exercise helps our metabolism and circulation. It can increase muscle mass to help our bodies become physically stronger. And if we are middle-aged, it helps our bodies fight against diabetes, heart disease, and strokes. We know that exercise releases chemicals in the brain that helps people battle discouragement. Endorphins and dopamine help our brain feel happy.

God wants us to have a positive self-esteem and to feel good about ourselves. There are specific assignments that God has for all of us, and those assignments will require us to shine the light of God's love on others and to speak out with boldness those things that God tells us to say. If God is prompting us to exercise, then He knows it will help us be ready for the assignments He has for us.

Diet

Being overweight isn't necessarily a sign that a person overeats. Some people may have metabolism or hormone issues. As well, some people are more genetically predisposed to carry extra weight. With that being said, most people that are overweight don't eat right.

For many people, the constant struggle to lose weight has been overwhelming for them. So, millions of people have simply stopped trying. They have given up and they have allowed themselves to become obese. While attempting to lose weight is a hassle, it is important to keep at it. It is better to try to diet and fail than to not try at all. When a person has given up all efforts to moderate their intake of food, they may soon find themselves very obese and very unhealthy. Obesity invites several types of ailments, and it can severely impact a person's quality of life.

Showing discipline with moderate portions is a key to weight loss, but another key is making better choices about the types of foods we put in our bodies. Limiting the amount of sugar, carbs, soda, fried foods, coffee, and processed foods can make a huge impact on our health.

Most of us hate the idea of showing discipline with what we eat. It is interesting that the Bible implies that we can gain spiritual strength when we control our food intake. If we were to do a web search of the spiritual benefits of fasting, we would find several Christian authors teaching on it. Some benefits are: 1) It helps us tune our spiritual ears to hear from God better. 2) Fasting demonstrates to God that our desire for Him is stronger than our desire for food. 3) Fasting our flesh nature makes us more spiritually minded where we can give more attention to the gifts and fruits of the spirit. 4) Putting our flesh nature under subjection gives our faith stronger muscles to conquer challenges in the spirit realm. 5) And disciplining our carnal nature causes the kingdom of darkness to respect us in the spirit realm.

So, while our carnal nature does not like the idea of being denied food, it can be extremely beneficial to our physical, emotional, and spiritual well-being.

Addictions

People can have addictions to alcohol, drugs, gambling, sex, food, and really almost anything. An addiction isn't just a bad habit. Addictions can seem like a compulsion where the person feels driven to engage in the activity. They, often times, feel like they have lost their own willful decision-making power over a vice, and they believe they must obey the drive within them. Addictions can also have a physical demand. For example, alcoholics and drug addicts can literally get sick if their addiction isn't satisfied.

Why do some people develop addictions while others don't? Psychology tells us that those people with addictive tendencies get more pleasure from the vice than other people do. Their brain is wired in such a way that they get rushes of positive feelings and feel-good chemicals released in their brain when they first start engaging in their vice. The areas of the brain responsible for stress and self-control undergo changes as well which contributes to their difficult in abstaining from the addictive substance or habit. Once the user gets used to the vice, the pleasure of it disappears and they need it just to feel normal.

I talked about neurological pathways earlier in this book. When we repeat behaviors, new neurological pathways are developed in our brain, and they become our go-to behaviors. An addict's brain has pathways that tell them that their addiction is their normal. Developing a new normal neurological pathway without their vice is possible but it is more difficult for them than it would be for a person without an addictive pull.

Our Speech

Most people don't control what they say. They express the random thoughts that roll through their minds regardless of the damage they may cause. Not showing discipline in what we say can: 1) damage reputations, 2) cause emotional harm, and 3) curse ourselves and others.

The book of Proverbs is full of verses that warn us about not controlling what we say. A high percentage of people just talk too much, and those people are usually unaware of the damage that they cause. Not only do they show their ignorance, but they also demean themselves and others. A mature person knows how to control their tongue.

I know people that say extremely mean and hurtful things when they are mad. They were never taught to fight fair in arguments and as a result, they emotionally wound people when they argue. They somehow think that their ugly comments are justified and acceptable because they were said in anger. Regardless of an apology later, some words can't be unspoken, and some harm can't be undone.

The average person curses themselves and others all the time. There is a spiritual world around us at all times that beckon to our words.

Whether we realize it or not, we give permission to demonic forces to harm us by the words that come out of our mouths. We invite chaos, sickness, and trouble into our lives and the lives of others when we prophesy and proclaim negative things into the atmosphere.

But just like demonic activity can be activated by what we say, angelic activity can as well. Palms 103:20 says, *"Bless the Lord, you His angels, who excel in strength, who do His word, heeding the voice of His word."* When we speak God's word over our situations, it activates angels to go to work to perform God's word in our lives. So, all of us need to get in the habit of speaking blessings and not curses over our lives and the lives of others.

Time Management

Most people misappropriate time on occasion but for some people, they do it constantly. Most people know or have known someone who always seems to be late. I used to know someone like that. She would ask me to pick her up at 9:30 am for a 10 am appointment. But when I got there, she wasn't ready and had two more calls to make before she finished getting dressed. We were an hour late to her appointment and her only comment was, "I did everything I could." No, she didn't. She was lying to me, and she was lying to herself. If I dared to mention her tardiness, she got flustered and frustrated at me. She was bad at budgeting her time. She would get caught up with something, lose track of time, then end up being late to everything scheduled that day.

Being late is not only a lack of discipline, it can also be a manifestation of pride. Being late tells the party that is waiting for you that they are not important. It tells them that you don't respect their time. The person that is always late is usually narcissistic, selfish, and they don't take the time to consider how their actions can impact others. Their tardiness demonstrates inconsiderate and selfish behavior.

Being late can also be a manifestation of self-sabotage. A person who is afraid of success or afraid of change, can subconsciously sabotage opportunities because their fear is trying to hamper their success.

As well, a person that carries unforgiveness towards themselves can also subconsciously use tardiness to sabotage opportunities.

It surprises me that most people that have a problem with time management are so casual about it. To them, it isn't a big deal, and they don't see a need for adjustment. The inability to show discipline in time management can be a rooted in a soul iniquity of weak willpower.

Money

Earlier in this book, I mentioned the *I need money* glitch that some people have that affects their behavior with money. However, some money wasters just lack discipline in the area of spending. For them, it isn't necessarily an autopilot response; it is more of an impulse control issue. They know rent will be due, but they make a choice to spend money on something they want now. Their lack of financial management demonstrates irresponsibility and inconsideration. People in that situation tend to rationalize that they could always borrow money that they will need later from a family member or friend. Making that assumption is a selfish behavior. It would mean another person will be asked to make sacrifices in their life, just so they can waste money on something they want now.

Cleaning

When it comes to house cleaning, people will gravitate towards the level of cleanliness that has been established in their subconscious comfort zone. I have known many *neat-freaks* and I have known many *slobs*.

My best friend in the early 90's was a married woman in her mid-30's. She used to keep her house immaculate. She wasn't O.C.D. about house cleaning. Surprisingly, she didn't appear to get upset if something got dirty. She was just very quick to clean it. I don't remember ever seeing a dirty dish in her sink. Dishes were immediately rinsed off and put in the dishwasher. She would also dust her furniture and vacuum her carpet every day. We worked at the same company and if I followed her home after work because we were planning on going out that night, she would always vacuum first. I questioned her about it one time. I said, "Why are you vacuuming the living room and family room? The rooms look perfect. You still see the vacuum rows in the carpet from yesterday." She said it's just something she has to do, and it would only take her a quick minute. She had no kids or pets and her husband had been gone all day at work. When her husband finally did get home, he would probably eat dinner in the kitchen, then go upstairs and watch TV in their bedroom. He probably wouldn't even see the two rooms she vacuumed but that didn't matter to her. She wasn't doing it for her husband. She is doing it because that was her programming in her subconscious mind. She was in the habit of cleaning her house everyday so that is what she did regardless of how busy her day was.

I have also known a few hoarders in my life. In 2003, a friend of mine asked me to help a friend of hers that was going to lose her condo through foreclosure. The woman literally slept in the garage because the two-bedroom condo was full of stuff. The front room had a narrow path to walk but the rest of it was piled high at least five feet tall. There wasn't enough time to clean it out and put it on the market before the set foreclosure date. I ended up quickly buying it below market value so at least the woman could walk away with some money. I had a crew loading junk into dumpsters for several days. It is hard to imagine that all that clutter was her comfort zone.

I had a roommate one time that was also a hoarder. She didn't have pizza boxes and chicken bones all over her room, but she did have stacks and stacks of boxes and papers. She frequently said she was cleaning her room, but she wasn't cleaning. She was sorting. She would go through her collection of papers, look at them and then put them right back into her "keep" stack. She wouldn't throw anything away.

The cleaning comfort zone isn't that hard to change. It is just a matter of starting out with a clean slate and them maintaining it. If you make yourself maintain a tidy room for a few weeks, it will become easier to change the cleanliness border in your subconscious mind.

Manifestations of Weak Willpower

Procrastination and Rationalization

Procrastination and rationalization are two of the most common manifestations of a lack of discipline. We lie to ourselves all the time. We aren't being disobedient. We'll just do it tomorrow. We make excuses and always find reasons why we can't do the task now. We may blame others, stay busy, and point to external obstacles as the hinderance.

People who procrastinate and rationalize tend to lack faithfulness and consistency. Employers can't count on them. They always have excuses for being late or absent. If money is lent to them, they hardly ever pay it back. They have gotten into the habit of giving themselves too much grace. Their word means nothing because they never do what they say they will do. People who have a stronghold of no self-discipline often lie to themselves and others and they don't realize how flaky their behavior is.

Erratic Behavior

Some people with self-discipline weaknesses have erratic behavior. They can have an *all or nothing* personality and can be unpredictable. They can easily be swept up into get rich schemes. Additionally, people with erratic behavior usually lack the discipline to complete courses they sign up for or projects that originate. They typically are not faithful in the little things, yet they expect to receive great responsibility and authority.

Secrecy

A need for secrecy can be a sign that there is a lack of discipline in someone's life. People hide their vices. They may hide food wrappers or empty vodka bottles. People with a weak willpower don't want to be exposed or judged so they hide their indulgences.

Closing Thoughts

Most people could improve in the area of self-discipline. Our carnal, flesh nature doesn't like to be put under subjection because it wants to rule our lives. However, demonstrating self-discipline improves our lives and can make our health, emotions, and spiritual life much better. Whereas a lack of discipline can cause significant harm to our lives in every way.

Romans 8:1, *"There is therefore now no condemnation to those who are in Christ Jesus, who do not walk according to the flesh, but according to the spirit."* So even though there is no condemnation from God, there can be conviction from God when He is directing us to correct a negative behavior pattern. Our objective should be to walk in the guidance and direction of the Holy Spirit and not aimlessly follow our fleshly, carnal desires. God is a God of grace, but we need to make sure we don't take God's grace for granted.

Thirteen

Sexual Sin, Addictions, and Fetishes

Human sexuality has always been a controversial subject. Through the ages, different cultures have responded differently to the matter. The Pilgrims and the Puritans never spoke about it, except behind closed doors, and only as a necessity for those who were about to marry. While the hippies of the 60's and 70's talked about it freely and practiced it liberally without restraint.

Various cultures and generations have held different practices and standards for human sexuality, but God hasn't. The Bible tells us that sex should only be practiced inside the covenant of marriage. God know us and He knows that being intimate with the wrong people can delay or abort the plans He has for our lives. Below are some other damaging affects it can have:

1) Degrades Intimacy. God intended sexual intimacy to be a sacred act between a husband and wife that would increase emotional intimacy and trust. Sex outside of marriage cheapens that covenant and degrades what God had intended for physical intimacy to be.

2) Creates Soul Ties. Sex creates a spiritual and emotional tie between two people. When we are intimate with someone that isn't our husband or wife, we create a bond with the wrong person. If we have a soul tie with the wrong person, that person may occupy our thoughts, pop up in our dreams, and even have the power to manipulate us in certain situations. We may obsess over them and be jealous when their attention is on someone else. We may know in our head that they are not the right person for us, but our heart feels connected to them.

3) Marry the Wrong Person. Because a bond is developed with physical intimacy, it is easy for a person to fall in love and believe the one they are with is the right one for them. A person's discernment is flawed when they are in love and their emotions trick them into believing the man or woman they are with is Mr. Right or Miss Right. A person can completely mess up God's plan for their life by marrying the wrong person.

4) Creates Drama. When people are physically intimate and they have a falling away, there is usually drama. Both parties are emotionally hurt, and they express that hurt and anger in different ways. They may lash out at the other person, try to harm their reputation, or attack them in other ways. A messy break-up can ruin a person's life.

5) Creates Baggage. A person that has been hurt in relationships usually carries those hurts into their next relationship. Wrong relationships create emotional baggage that people carry from one relationship to the other. Those old emotional scars can trigger surprising and unwarranted reactions to perfectly innocent comments or actions. Without realizing it, a person can attach some of the emotional pain from their last relationship into their current one.

God gave us the guideline that sex is supposed to be within marriage to protect us from emotional harm. Even though sex is a physical act, it touches our soul. It can make imprints in our subconscious mind. If we experience rejection or emotional abuse in relationships, it can imprint on our subconscious mind and do substantial harm to our self-esteem.

The Sex Drive

A person's sex drive, or libido, can be affected by several factors. Some people are just genetically predisposed with a stronger sex drive, while others are not. But most people's libido is affected by their age, hormone levels, physical health, and emotional well-being. Age obviously has a bearing, with males peaking sexually in their late teens and females peak in their mid-30's. Hormone levels play a huge role in people's desire for sex and their sexual aptitude. As men grow older, their testosterone levels go down and low testosterone lowers a man's desire for sex and even his ability to have sex. As women age, their estrogen and progesterone levels decrease, and their libido usually decreases as well. The physical health of a person can also impact their sex drive. If a person is obese, has cancer, diabetes, an under-active thyroid, liver or kidney disease, backpain, nerve damage, heart problems, or vascular weakness, it usually lowers their sexual desire and performance. Emotional health issues like stress, anxiety, and depression can also affect a person. And a person's self-esteem can have a huge bearing on how sexy they feel. If someone feels attractive, they will, most likely, feel in the mood more often than someone who isn't happy with themselves. As well, if a man is drunk, his ability to have sex greatly decreases.

It is not uncommon for a spouse to feel rejected if their mate doesn't want to have sex as often as they do. What many of them don't realize is it usually isn't a personal rejection of their husband or wife. Their disinterest in sex is probably because of one of the factors mentioned above.

In the early 90's, I was friends with a married couple. The wife felt rejected because her husband's libido was low. He only wanted sex once every month or two. She took this as a personal rejection and actually went out and had affairs on him because she wanted to feel sexually desirable. She wasn't a sex addict. It wasn't about physical pleasure to her. It was about her self-esteem. She had to prove to herself that she was still desirable to the opposite sex. Her husband found her attractive, but he had Low T (low testosterone) and didn't know it. If we knew then what we know now, their marriage could have been saved.

Forty percent of men over 45 years old have Low T. This affects their sexual features, muscle mass, level of red blood cells, bone density, sense of well-being, and their sexual and reproductive function. Men can take testosterone replacement and they can take sexual performance drugs if they are healthy enough for them. So, having Low T doesn't necessarily mean they don't get to have an active sex life with their wife.

Sexual function tends to be important to men and many men base their whole ego around it. However, I will say this, before spending a lot of time and money on hormone therapies and enhancement pills, check in with your wife. Depending on her age and libido level, frequent sex, or sex at all may not be a priority to her. She may just want to be close to her husband but that doesn't mean that it has to be sexual.

How Sexual Attraction Works

If we were to look at the science of attraction, we would find that there are different brain chemicals released with each type or stage of attraction. There are three types: 1) lust, 2) attraction, and 3) attachment. These three types can be stages of the same relationship, or they can be types that not all relationships experience.

When lust is present, the hormones testosterone and estrogen are produced. This type of desirability is only about physical attraction. The allure is solely based on sexual function and lust hormones. The sexual desire for the person doesn't care about their personality, sense of humor, or character.

The second type is attraction. The brain chemicals dopamine and norepinephrine are produced in this state and there is a reduction of serotonin. These chemicals make a person feel giddy, energetic, euphoric, and can even lead to a decreased appetite and insomnia. This type of attraction is the puppy love stage of a relationship. These puppy love attractions tend to be based on more than just appearance. There is usually something about the other person's persona that we may be drawn to. Sometimes we know what it is that draws us and sometimes we don't. With attraction, it can happen instantly or over time. It can grow if there is an emotional connection. A person's intelligence, kindness, or sense of humor may get the other person's attention. When a person is in the attraction stage of a relationship, they are usually wearing rose colored glasses. They can't see the faults of their new love interest so they may be attracted to the wrong person. They can feel totally in love with a person that is completely wrong for them. Relationship junkies love this type of relationship. They love feeling the in love emotional highs. But they usually bail out when the rose-colored glasses fall off and they see the flaws of the other person or when those brain chemicals fade.

And finally, the third type of attraction is attachment. This type of relationship produces the brain chemicals oxytocin and vasopressin. These chemicals are often called the "cuddle hormones." The attachment hormones are present when you have a significant other, but they can also be present with your children, family, and close friends. The attachment stage of a relationship is characterized by feelings of calm, security, social comfort, and emotional union. At this stage, the couple is a united front. They have each other's back and they function as a team. The union is happy and secure.

What People Find Attractive Changes

It has been said that sex is 95% mental and only 5% physical. I don't know if those percentages are correct, but I would agree that sexuality is mostly mental. The feelings of the three types of attraction are all based out of chemicals in the brain.

Why do married couples fall out of love? Why do the attachment brain chemicals stop their production, so the couple no longer has *that lovin' feeling*? The responsibility really rests on both people.

A person can choose what they focus on. If we concentrate on the positive stuff, the right attachment chemicals will continue to be produced in the brain. If someone is constantly mad at their spouse, there will not be any positive love chemicals produced in their brain and it will damage the relationship.

Philippians 4:8 says, *"Finally, brethren, whatever things are true, whatever things are noble, whatever things are just, whatever things are pure, whatever things are lovely, whatever things are of a good report, if there is any virtue and if there is anything praiseworthy – meditate on these things."* This verse is the secret to a happy marriage. If we make it a practice to focus on and think about the positive stuff about our spouse, then the little annoyances won't bug us as much.

Likewise, if we are married, we shouldn't make our spouse try to conjure up old memories of when we were nice, kind, or romantic. We should practice those things all the time. Try to keep the flirt in the relationship. Be nice to each other and say nice things. Don't underestimate the affect that little things can have. We don't have to do big romantic gestures. Sometimes, just holding our significant other's hand can spark love chemicals in the brain.

If we want our spouse to think of us as true, noble, just, pure, and lovely, then we need to be true, noble, just, pure, and lovely. Are we being true? Do we lie or act shady? Not being able to trust our husband or wife stops the *lovey-dovey* chemicals and emotions faster than most other things. If we want a good spouse, then we need to be a good spouse.

It always surprises me when a husband or wife tries to make the other jealous. That doesn't endear a person; it creates distrust and drives them away.

As far as the initial attraction is concerned, what goes on in our mind and subconscious mind are what determines who we are attracted to. Of course, there are people that are considered beautiful and handsome, but that doesn't mean that we are specifically drawn to those people. A person can be attracted to someone for many different reasons. We can be drawn to a person's persona, mannerisms, and how they carry themselves - not just their appearance. We may notice little things about someone that are subtle and endearing to us but would be meaningless to others. Our mind can store a dozen snapshots of glances, vocal infections, and expressions that we compile in our memory when we start to develop a crush on someone.

Beauty is very much in the eye of the beholder. A person may have a specific type that they are attracted to. There are men that are only attracted to very thin women and there are men that are only attracted to very heavy women. For some men, it isn't the size of the woman; it's how she carries herself. For many women, a man's looks are not the biggest factor in their attraction to them. Some women are more attracted to intelligence, humor, wealth, or prestige rather than a simply handsome man.

Even as far as what society deems as attractive has changed over the decades and centuries. In the 1500's, being fat with fair-skinned was viewed as beautiful. Look at the art from that time period. The nude paintings of women showed them with small breasts but with a fat belly, hips, and legs. They were pear-shaped but apparently that was a good thing back then. In the 70's, women had to have blond hair, a dark tan, and look like Farah Faucet. In early 80's, men had to have the Tom Selleck mustache and a hairy chest to be considered sexy. In the 2020's, men are supposed to have hairless bodies to be considered sexy. So, what society views as attractive does change quite often.

Reader discretion is advised – This next section may not be suitable for all readers. If you are uncomfortable discussing human sexuality in greater detail, I suggest you skip the rest of this chapter.

I read a very interesting book in 2006 entitled, *Sex, Men and God* by Douglas Weiss, who is a licensed psychologist, specializing in the treatment of sexual addiction and "intimacy anorexics." The book details how men develop their attractions and fetishes.

He told a story of a man that had a boot fetish. Boots got him sexually excited. He had boots tacked up on the walls of his bedroom because it heightened his sexual experiences. We discover in the book that he developed that boot fetish when he was an adolescent in his first couple of years of puberty. He lived in the country in a small cabin with other family members. When the boy wanted to masturbate, he had to do it away from his house. So, he would put on his boots and walked behind the outhouse to pleasure himself. It was dark out. There was nothing to look at. So, he used to stare at his boots when he masturbated.

Douglas Weiss theorizes in his book that whatever a man looks at when he ejaculates, he bonds with, and that object or person will sexually excite them in the future. The boy stared at his boots when he masturbated, so it turned into a fetish for him. He goes on to suggest that when husbands and wives have sex, that they do it with the lights on, looking at each other. He says this will help create the bond for the man to only be attracted to his wife. He said to never allow fantasies to creep in because that can damage the bond between husband and wife.

Porn

I believe Doug Weiss' conclusions are correct and can be proven when we look at the area of pornography. I have known more than one couple where the husband was addicted to porn, and the husband couldn't have sex with his wife.

In 2004, I was the guest speaker at a church that was two counties away. At the end of the service, there was a time of altar ministry. I had a prophetic word for a woman as I was praying for her. The word was that God delighted in her, He was head-over-heels in love with her, and

He loves their time together. God wanted me to tell her that she needed to stop blaming herself for a situation she is in. She needed to release it to God and stop allowing condemnation to attack her mind.

The woman told me after the service that her husband was addicted to porn and that he masturbated to it seven or eight times a day. She didn't know what to do. Her husband wouldn't have sex with her and only wanted porn. She blamed herself, with thoughts of not being pretty enough or skinny enough to interest her husband. She felt lonely, undesirable, and heart broken. The prophetic word that was given to her was like water to someone in the desert who was dying of thirst. The word brought emotional healing which she desperately needed in that season of her life.

It wasn't the woman's fault. There wasn't something wrong with her. The problem was her husband's addiction to pornography that caused him to bond with porn stars and their lady parts. He physically couldn't be sexually aroused by his wife because he was only sexually aroused to porn. Certainly, in this case, Doug Weiss' theory on sexual bonding was true.

Porn is a $97 billion dollar industry globally, with about $13 billion coming from the United States. Porn is a huge industry that is detrimental to society for several reasons.

The first reason is that it causes sexual problems in marriages, as demonstrated by the story above. If a man exclusive engages in porn long enough, it can get to the point where he can't get an erection with his wife.

Another reason why porn is harmful is that it objectifies women. A man's brain can disconnect from God's original intent for sex if he views too much porn. God created sex to be a pleasurable, intimate exchange that increased a couple's emotional and spiritual bond. And, of course, it was designed for procreation. However, objectifying women to be mere channels for sexual pleasure for the man, minimizes their position and place in society. By bonding with body parts, instead of with the person they love and respect, a man's brain can reroute neurological pathways and view women in a disrespectful way. Without even consciously being aware of it, women will start to hold a lower level of respect in a man's heart. Perhaps women won't be treated as poorly as they are in Muslim countries, but they won't carry the same value, reverence, and admiration as a man. It may be unspoken and, most likely, not recognized, but the objectification of women diminishes how women are viewed in the workplace and in society.

And finally, the third reason porn damages our society is that it is an addiction for many people. According to a survey by www.church-militant.com in 2016, Christian men view porn almost as much as non-Christian men.

"According to the research, approximately 64%, or two thirds, of U.S. men admit to viewing porn at least monthly, with the number of Christian men nearly equaling the national average. When divided by age, eight out of ten (79%) men between the ages of 18 and 30 view pornography at least monthly, and two thirds (67%) of men between the ages of 31 and 49 view pornography at least monthly. One half (50%) of men between 50 and 68 looks at porn monthly."

"In terms of addiction or perceived addiction, 13 percent of all men questioned admitted to having an addiction to pornography, with another 5 percent claiming they are unsure. The numbers among Christian men are higher, as 2 in 10 men of no specific age group believe themselves to be addicted or are not sure."

So that study published in January of 2016 tells us that 64% of men watch porn and that 20% of Christian men think they are addicted to porn. As well, that article stated that approximately 20% of women watch porn at least once a month, so it is a widespread issue.

Sexual Fluidity

Is being gay genetic? Well, it depends what article you read. Some scientists say that there are two genes linked to sexual orientation that are located on chromosomes 13 and 14. While other scientists rebuff their claims and say their evidence is too weak to state that theory as fact.

If we look at LGBTQ community by age group, we see a great disparity. According to the Gallup poll, between 2% and 3% of baby boomers (born between 1946 and 1964) and Generation X (born between 1965 and 1979) identify in the LGBTQ community. Whereas it is much higher for the Millennials (born between 1980 and 1994) and Gen Z (born between 1995 and 2012). One survey showed that 20% of Millennials were LGBTQ, while another study showed that roughly 30% of Gen Z and Millennials were within the LGBTQ community.

Certainly, we don't jump from 2% to 30% if it is just genetic. It goes without saying that the LGBTQ community would proclaim that 30% of people have always been gay or bi-sexual but they were just repressed until now. While the conservative, heterosexual community would say that the LGBTQ, working with education, media, and the entertainment industry have taught children to be experimental and to not have sexual boundaries. They would site evidence of how children have been groomed for gender and sexual fluidity all under the guise of anti-discrimination.

I believe the majority of a person's lifestyle choices are taught in childhood. That is not to say that the chromosome thing isn't valid. It may very well be, but for like 2%, not 30%. I also acknowledge there can be other influences that sway a person towards homosexuality besides what they are taught. It is not uncommon for a boy that was sexually molested to lean towards the gay or bi lifestyle. Women that have been hurt by men, have transitioned over to a lesbian life. And statistically, some boys who grew up with overbearing mothers turn to the LGBTQ life. So, it is fair to say that certain situations may influence a person's sexual attractions.

Why are 30% of Millennials and Gen Z-ers part of the LGBTQ community? Because many of the governments of the world have made it almost illegal to say sex should be between a man and a woman. We have two generations that have been taught to experiment sexually and that everything is good as long as all parties' consent. Preachers can't talk about sex from the pulpit, or they will be blasted on social media, fined, or in some cases arrested. No one is allowed to have an opinion unless that opinion is in favor of gender and sexual fluidity.

I know a lesbian that was raised in a Christian home but as an adolescent was caught fornicating with a boy. Apparently, she had an active sex life in her young teen years. She got severely reprimanded. I think the message that "sex with the boy was bad," sunk down into her subconscious mind, so much so that the lesbian thing blossomed as a substitute. Some people would theorize that the substitution thing is why some priests molest altar boys. Their mind and their subconscious mind have been conditioned to not have sex with women, so they gravitate towards a substitute.

Everyone's story may be a little different and we can't make broad stroke generalizations. However, the later generations have a much easier time engaging in sexual fluidity because they weren't taught the borders and boundaries that earlier generations were taught.

If we look at Doug Weiss' theory as it applies to these later generations, it makes sense. Doug Weiss concluded that over time, a person will bond with whatever they are looking at when they reach a sexual climax. Millennials and Gen Z-ers were taught to masturbate at an early age and to be open minded. The negative stigma was removed from masturbation, so it was practiced as soon as a preteen started to have sexual feelings. Well, most boys looked at their penis while masturbating so it is within reason that many of them formed an attraction to the penis. And some girls probably masturbated while looking in a mirror. I would image that most of them didn't close their eyes and they fantasized or watched porn. They stared at themselves and in doing so, may have opened the door to some gay or bi-sexual tendencies.

Lust

Regardless of the generation we were born into, we always have a choice not to engage in sexual activity. Compared to some of the other topics in this chapter, lust may not even seem like it can be a sin.

Lust is a very strong sexual desire. It is a stirring for sex with someone in one's imagination to the point that they will think about it and even fantasize about it.

If the sexual thought isn't acted out, is it even wrong? Yes. Jesus compared lust to adultery in Matthew 5:28. The verse reads, *"But I say to you that whoever looks at a woman to lust for her has already committed adultery with her in his heart."*

Having sexual thoughts is normal and expected depending on your age. But meditating on those thoughts and fantasizing about sexual acts with a certain person is wrong. You are, in essence, violating her in your thought life.

Fornication

Most of the time, fornication is a by-product of lust but not all the time. It is not uncommon for women to have sex because they are trying to please their new boyfriends. They may fear rejection, loneliness, and/or abandonment so they consent to have sex.

While fear of abandonment does happen, most of the time fornication happens because two people are feeling sexual. A Christian woman I know felt the need to confess her sexual escapades to me when I really didn't want to know them. She told me she went on a road trip with a man. She described how they had accidently started kissing and before she knew it, they were at the "point of no return."

The notion that there is a "point of no return" is a lie. People lie to themselves when they say that once their flesh is worked up, they can't stop. By thinking they have reached the "point of no return," they give themselves permission to go all the way.

People don't just fall into fornication. They plan for it. Why was the woman taking a road trip alone with a man? You can't say that she didn't know that something was going to happen. Why would she actively engage in heavy kissing and petting if she wasn't planning on having sex? If someone really didn't want to have sex, why wouldn't they stop themselves after the first kiss? Or why would they start kissing at all?

Adultery

Like fornication, adultery doesn't just happen. And like with lust, scenarios are usually played out in the imagination before anything actually happens. Both people convince themselves that the little glances and flirtatious gestures are just for fun and that nothing would come of it. Those little flirtations feed their self-esteem because it feels good to be desired.

If actions are not taken to stop all flirtations, a person can soon find themselves in a precarious position. Once a married person recognizes that they have chemistry with another person and some flirtations have happened, they need to take quick actions to stop it in its track. They need to mentally treat the flirtation like a snake that snuck into the house. They need to get their broom and push it out the door. That doesn't mean that they need to have an awkward conversation with the other person. They may be able to stop the chemistry by simply stopping themselves from flirting and doing something non-verbally that shows the person that they are rejecting the flirtations. Usually, the other person will sense a wall going up and soon, they will put up their wall too.

Incest/Molestation

According to Wikipedia, 19.7% of girls and 7.9% of boys are sexually abused. Most sexual offenders are acquainted with the victims, with approximately 30% being related to the child (brothers, fathers, uncles, and cousins), around 60% are acquaintances (friends of the family, babysitters, and neighbors) and 10% of the abuses happen by strangers.

Numerous studies have been done detailing the psychological and even physical damage it can cause. The level of damage typically depends on the level of the abuse and who the abuser was to the victim.

With roughly 20% of girls and 8% of boys being abused, it would suggest that as high as 10% to 28% of adults are sexual pedophiles. That is a huge number. Think of all the dysfunctional families that are affected by this evil secret. Think of all the men that carry around guilt for harming children. How many of those men are Christians that have justified their behavior, thinking it really doesn't do that much damage? On the other side of the coin, how many of those men carry secret guilt and embrace self-sabotaging behaviors because they don't feel worthy of forgiveness or success?

Sadistic/Masochistic Behavior

S & M is a thriving practice. There are special sex clubs and online rooms that showcase a dominatrix with a willing, subservient participant. Sadistic behavior means a person is very cruel or that a person takes sexual pleasure in inflicting pain, punishment, or humiliation on others. While a masochistic person derives pleasure from abuse, punishment, humiliation, and being dominated.

A sadistic person is usually mean and controlling both in the bedroom and in their real life. They are usually angry and vulgar, and they have been known to criticize others relentlessly. They strive to humiliate as part of their normal routine.

A masochistic person usually has high standards of success. They are a perfectionist that constantly falls short of the standard they have set for themselves. It is perceived that masochistic people come from a "battle of will" between the developing child and an over-controlling parent. They require obedience and compliance all the time. The person is drawn into situations and relationships in which they will suffer and prevent others from helping them.

Fetishes

In a moment, I will list some fetishes I saw online. I have to say I had never heard of the majority of them. When you read the descriptions,

I am sure you will agree with me that many of these are purely demonic. To practice some of them is inviting demons into the bedroom and certainly it is a place where the demons in a person are allowed to express themselves.

The following is a list of fetishes:

Spanking, role-playing, foot fetish, anal fetish, lingerie, group sex, sensation play (blindfold, ice), bondage, voyeurism (watching others), exhibitionism (others watching you), spectrophilia (means sex with ghosts but is really sex with demons), autonepiophilia (adults dress and act like babies), Urophilia (urinating on each other), wax play, vorarephilia (getting turned on by mock cannibalism), quirofilia (attraction to hands), pregnancy (attraction to pregnant women), tentacles (attraction for octopus tentacles), age play (pretending your partner is your daddy, mommy, or child), stranger play, emetophilia (one gets aroused by vomit), klismaphilia (aroused by enemas), and electrostimulation (using electricity for sexual purposes).

Bestiality

Writing in the 1940's, famed sexual researcher Alfred Kinsey estimated that 8% of men and 3.6% of women had engaged in some sort of sexual act with an animal. There was a later study by Morton M. Hunt in 1974, that said the percentage of men that have sex with animals is 4.9%, and 1.9% of women do as well.

In the U.S., bestiality is illegal in 31 states, with 16 states labeling it as a felony, and 15 as a misdemeanor. Dogs and cows are the animals most often used in sexual acts.

A new term has been created for those people that have ongoing sexual relationships with animals and that term is *zoosexual*. There are zoosexual clubs and apparently even zoosexual parties.

Sex Issues as a *Disease of the Soul*

Just because someone has an active libido doesn't mean that they have a soul iniquity of sex sin. God created humans to be sexual beings, but that sexuality is supposed to be expressed inside the borders of marriage and nowhere else.

Christians can evaluate themselves to determine whether or not they have a *disease of the soul* of sexual sin. You can have sexual sin in your life without having a subconscious stronghold. A couple can be living together, having sex before marriage but that doesn't mean that one or both of them have a sex soul iniquity in their subconscious mind.

A person with a soul iniquity of sexual sin has challenges with their self-control. A husband that is a serial cheater may point to the flaws of his wife as the problem, but his compulsion for affairs would be evidence that he has a sexual stronghold.

Some sexual depravity is obviously demonic and sometimes a person doesn't just cooperate with demons, but they have a demon living in their subconscious mind as a *disease of the soul*. Some sex demons are itty bitty ones and other ones are big, evil monsters. In my opinion, a demon has to be involved for a grown man to rape a child. To strip that child of their innocence, knowing it can permanently damage their psyche, is pure evil.

In the Weak Willpower chapter, it was mentioned that a person's level of self-control is what determines if that issue is a *disease of the soul* or not. I believe the same is true in this chapter as well. In the area of sexuality and all its variants, do you have self-control? Are you in charge of your actions or are you obeying an insatiable drive? If you can't stop any activity cold turkey, then it is likely a stronghold.

Closing Thoughts

This chapter talked about stages of attraction and brain chemicals that are released with each one. It encouraged you to meditate on the positive qualities of your husband or wife rather than focusing on the things that bug you.

If there are areas of sexual sin that require repentance, don't skip it just because you realize it will probably happen again. Each time an issue is surrendered to God, the closer you will be to conquering it. Don't fall in the trap of thinking you are powerless over an area of your life. That is a lie from the dark side. You *"can do all things through Christ who strengthens"* you (Philippians 4:13). Repent, and practice good morals.

Fourteen

Idolatry

When most of us think of idolatry, we think of the children of Israel in the desert when Moses went up the mountain to get the Ten Commandments and the people built a golden cow to worship. We, oftentimes, dismiss the term *idolatry* because it seems like it doesn't exist in our current culture.

Idolatry happens when there is worship for something other than God or there is too much admiration for something or someone. Idolatry doesn't just happen in India where Hindus worship 1,000 gods, it happens here in the Western World as well. But the gods here aren't made of gold, stone, or wood. An idol can be anything we prioritize over God. The New Living Translation of 1 John 5:21 says, *"Dear children, keep away from anything that might take God's place in your heart."*

In October of 1996, I attended a Coldwell Banker Sales Training course, which was a two-week training designed to show real estate agents how to get new clients. The instructor that taught the sales portion of the training used the premise that: *You have to kiss a lot of frogs to find your prince.* She had frog figurines and frog stuffed animals all over the room. The frogs represented potential clients. She said one out of seven of the potential clients actually turns into real clients. She stressed the importance of working with a lot of prospective clients in order to build a strong client base.

During that season of my life, God frequently whispered a scripture reference to read along with my normal Bible reading. It didn't happen all the time, but a few times a week a Bible book and chapter number would come up in my spirit. When I turned to the passage, God would speak to my heart by giving me correction, direction, or affection.

On the Thursday morning of the sale training, I was prompted to read Psalm 2. As I read the chapter, the first part of verse 12 stood out to me. It said, "Kiss the Son." When I read that, the Holy Spirit said, "Kiss the Son and you won't have to kiss a lot of frogs." The basic meaning of that is found in Matthew 6:33 which says, *"But seek first the kingdom of God and His righteousness, and all these things shall be added to you."* God was telling me that if I put Him first, I wouldn't have to waste my time on non-productive projects and do-nothing potential clients. If I was going to spend time working with someone it was for a reason, either for them to do a real estate transaction or because God was going to use the appointment for His purposes.

God needs to come first in our life. Most of us would agree with that statement in principle, but our lives may reflect a different story. We may allow the lust of the eyes, the lust of the flesh, and the pride of life to take our focus off of God and put it somewhere else. Remember, if there is something or someone that we prioritize ahead of God, we are in idolatry.

Modern Day Idolatry

Before I discuss some of the various things we may prioritize over God, I want to address a type of idolatry that has risen up in the last half of century. It is the worship of self which has embedded itself with some of the New Age teachings. Much of the New Age ideologies were birthed in idolatry. It is men trying to prove that they themselves are gods.

I would agree with the New Agers that teach that humans don't fully understand the spiritual power they carry and that they don't tap into the potential that lies dormant within them. God has equipped mankind to walk in much more spiritual power and authority than we practice. We are hardwired by God with the ability to move mountains and raise the dead. It is our birthright as Christians, but most believers don't understand faith enough to even attempt either of these two things. However, the New Age beliefs put too much emphasis on self, instead of on God. It teaches a philosophy of worshipping the created instead of the creator.

Recently, the scripture reference of John 4 came up in my spirit, so I read it. That chapter talks about when Jesus met the woman at the well who was a Samaritan. When I came to John 4:22, the Holy Spirit stopped me and spoke to me. The first part of the verse reads, *"You worship what you do not know."* After I read that, the Holy Spirit said, "This is what New Agers do." I wasn't thinking about the New Age religion at all but when I read the sentence again, I understood what God was trying to tell me.

New Agers glorify self, but they don't understand the weaknesses and iniquities that reside within the human psyche. They don't know that pride leads to deceptive thinking. They don't know that jealousy is a sin. They don't understand that the true motives of people are often hidden from their understanding because they are housed in the subconscious mind.

So, while some of their beliefs are valid, most of the New Agers live in the delusion of their own pride. It is only when we recognize the iniquities within us and actively work on uprooting those diseases out of our soul, that we will be in a position to flow in more spiritual authority. Our motives need to be right, and we need to be following God's guidance in order for us to reach spiritual plateaus. Our efforts are just folly if God isn't our sole focus.

Manifestations of Idolatry

Social Media

This may be a hard concept to hear but a large percentage of Christians are guilty of idolatry when it comes to social media. They used to read their Bibles but now they spend all their free time on social media. Social media has been a venue for preaching and words of edification for believers, but many Christians skip over those posts and view other content.

Social media doesn't have to be a bad thing but each of us need to make sure we don't skip time with God because of it. Set a routine for yourself that includes time with God without interruptions for texts, calls, email, or social media notifications.

Work

Most people don't like work, so how can it become an idol? Some jobs are busy, stressful, and extremely time consuming. I get that. There have been seasons of my life where I worked 12 or 13 hours a day but that is not sustainable. There may be times where a deadline is coming up and we need to work late, however, that shouldn't be the normal routine. We are the captains of our careers. We should make choices where we don't end up being a workaholic. Every waking moment, whether it's before work, at work, or when we get home, shouldn't be spent thinking about work related situations. If all our time is spent on work or worrying about work, then there is no time for God; and He isn't the first priority in our life.

A Relationship

Relationships are important. God created us to be social beings. In the Garden of Eden, God said it wasn't good that man should be alone, so He created Eve. Living in isolation is not emotionally healthy. However, we need to be cautious if a friendship or romantic relationship takes priority over our relationship with God. It is a good idea to examine the priority level of our relationships. Does our time with God get pushed aside so we can spend time with that other person?

I understand when two people first start dating and they are in that puppy love stage. They are infatuated with each other. When they have that mush brain, it is difficult for them to concentrate on their job or on their schoolwork if they are in school. The good news is that the puppy love stage usually lasts from one week to six months, so the brain fog of love won't last long. You will get your brain back! And believe it or not, a person can ask God to lessen the puppy love mush brain so they can function and think about other things besides their new boyfriend or girlfriend.

A Hobby

Hobbies are good. There is nothing wrong with having a hobby. But again, a person needs to keep themselves in check to make sure that hobby isn't the first priority in their life.

People can be obsessed with bird watching, train sets, stamp collecting, reading, martial arts, jewelry making, wood working, gardening, video games, fishing, yoga, traveling, golf, playing cards, board games, eating out (a foodie), tennis, dancing, painting, cooking, bicycling, movies, genealogy, podcast, TV, antiques or collectables, music, shopping, garage sales, etc. Almost any activity can become a hobby, which can turn into an obsession. Hobbies are not a bad thing. We just need to be careful they don't rob our lives of the truly important things.

Fitness

Exercise and fitness are important. However, there are people whose bodies have become their idol. They usually are in the gym daily and when they aren't in the gym, they are thinking about their body. They may obsess about getting their BMI just a little lower, or their biceps just a little bigger, or their waist just a little slimmer. Being obsessed about our bodies can make it an idol in our lives.

A Celebrity

Some people idolize other people. It's hard for me to wrap my head around it because I have never had a fascination with an actor or sports star, but some people have. Everyone is fallible. Everyone has positive and negative traits. Hero worship is not okay. It is good to admire people for their achievements but never put them on a high pedestal in your mind. They are human and if you saw their weaknesses, you wouldn't idolize them.

A Sport or Sports Team

Following a sport and having a favorite sports team can be fun. There is nothing wrong with looking forward to basketball, football, baseball, or soccer games. It is fun to gather friends and watch the Super Bowl or World Series. But obsessing over a sport too much isn't good. A game shouldn't be your god. There are some people that sacrifice their careers and family for a silly game. If someone obsesses more about a sport than the things of God, then they have an idol in their life.

Closing Thoughts

Idolatry seems like such an old fashion word and an old fashion concept. But just because it isn't discussed as much as it used to be, doesn't mean it doesn't exist. It seems like our modern-day churches ignore the whole topic, like it has somehow become okay with God. Idolatry is listed as the first two commandments in the Bible. 1) You shall have no other gods before me, and 2) You shall make no idols. That seems pretty clear that it is important to God. We need to keep ourselves in check to ensure that God always stays the first priority in our lives.

Fifteen

Greed/Selfish Ambition

Greed is an intense desire for something – usually wealth, power, or food. It can be similar to envy but it's more universal. It isn't just envying the possessions of a specific person. It is an unspecific quest for more. When someone is greedy, the money they have is never enough. There is an internal drive in them to always accumulate more.

Selfish ambition, like greed, also has that internal drive to always want more but it's more about power, prestige, and authority rather than possessions. Selfish ambition is about making a name for yourself. There is an intrinsic determination that compels a person to achieve more and obtain more fame, power, honor, or authority.

We are a society of people that live in fear and laziness. Most people lack any ambition. The average person achieves very little in their life because they have very little motivation to succeed. So, when we come across ambitious people, we honor and praise them for their internal fortitude. In a general sense, ambition is a good thing. It's a necessary attribute for successful people. Desiring success is a good thing because too many people sabotage their success. It's good to see when people are able to break out of their self-imposed comfort zones and achieve levels of success.

With all that said, we need to make sure our desire to succeed isn't rooted in the soul iniquity of greed. While we strive to succeed, we need to always be mindful of our actions. We need to ensure we are not hurting other people in our journey towards success.

Greed is an attitude of heart. People who have nothing can be greedy. In fact, in most cases, the people who have nothing are usually the ones who covet what others have. Greed is not measured by how much you have but rather by how much that stuff has you. Would you give up everything if God asked you to? In Matthew 19, Jesus tested the rich young ruler by asking him to give up all he had, but the rich man could not do it.

I believe that God often tests the hearts of His people. It has been my experience that before God blesses someone with wealth and prosperity, He orchestrates situations so that a person can see the condition of their own heart. In some cases, He takes them through a season of lack in order for them to learn firsthand how to lean on God as their provider and not their own wisdom. When Christians have learned by experience that they can find God's peace in the middle of a financial storm, they are empowered to defeat the fear. And when Christians have the right heart attitude towards money, God can trust them with financial prosperity.

Selfish ambition is like rebellion in that it can be a byproduct of another *disease of the soul.* A root of selfish ambition can spring up as a weed when other shrubs of iniquities drop their seeds in the fertile soil of a person's subconscious mind. For example, someone with a root of fear can develop greed to hoard material possessions. Or someone with pride can develop self-ambition because of their intrinsic drive to control situations. A person with a root of jealousy may develop selfish ambition in an effort to carry out their plans and disrupt the plans of the one they are jealous of. People may assume their personal motives are pure and may not know their actions are driven from a wrong motive. They may think they are acting on behalf of God when really, they are playing out their own agendas.

God is a big God. Even when people have wrong motives, God can work through them to accomplish His objectives. If everyone waited to have a pure heart before stepping out in ministry projects, nothing would get done. As we move forward in purging our hearts, we need to make sure we don't get so self-analytical that we stop our forward momentum.

Selfish Ambition in the Church

While a certain level of ambition is expected in the corporate world, it shouldn't exist in churches. Our culture is so saturated with self-promotion, it shouldn't be a surprise that it is prevalent in ministries as well. I am sure most churches have people competing for positions, whether that it is on the pastoral staff, or on the music team, or among the volunteers. People seek position, honor, and authority.

A while back, I was on a church leadership team. The pastor wanted to add more people to the group, so a member of the congregation was invited to join. A very pleasant woman with whom I had known as an acquaintance for many years was invited to be part of the group. She was added to the leadership team as an assistant to the department leader who oversaw greeters, alter workers, and hospitality.

At a service, the woman pulled some of the greeters aside and started training them in a new protocol. A greeter mentioned it to the department leader, so the department leader approached the woman to ask if there had been a change in leadership that she wasn't aware of. She wasn't asking to be confrontational or sarcastic; she genuinely wanted to know if the woman had been put in charge of the greeters. The woman didn't answer the question, instead she just stared at her. By her non-response, the department leader assumed the woman was put in charge and said she would gladly step aside. When the woman finally did talk, she said she had mentioned her protocol idea to the senior pastor, and he liked the idea. The woman implied that she was acting at the direction of the pastor. (Obviously, when the pastor said that he like her idea, he didn't intend for her to unseat the department head and train the greeters without the knowledge of the department leader.) The department leader said her life was busy, her ego didn't need the responsibility, and she didn't want to engage in any drama. So, she told the woman that she was fine passing the baton of head of the greeters to her.

And just like that, the woman bumped herself up the leadership ladder. To the outside observer, it might have seemed like a big misunderstanding. However, after hearing three sides of the story (from the woman, from the leader, and from a volunteer that witnessed the exchange), it was clear to me that the woman maneuvered and manipulated the power steal.

The situation seemed strange to me. I couldn't understand why the woman wanted that leadership position so much. It didn't come with a lot of prestige or honor. But as time went on, I understood more.

One day the Holy Spirit told me, "She is gathering her chicks." I understood that to mean the woman was playing mother hen to the greeters and setting herself up as a pastor figure in their lives. After that, I was approached by one of the greeters and she told me she was quitting as a greeter. She said that the woman calls all the greeters during the week, and it takes up too much of their time on long phone calls. The position didn't require a lot of communication with the greeters. A simple weekly text message would have been sufficient. The volunteers were spiritually mature women but apparently, the woman was trying to make them spiritually accountable to her. She was treating the greeter volunteers as her spiritual children and positioning herself as their spiritual superior.

After I finished the conversation with that greeter, the Holy Spirit told me, "She wants to be the Women's Pastor for the church." That surprised me. At that time, the woman who was the new greeter leader was also buddying up to the women's ministry pastor. But I didn't know that she wanted that position too.

Over the next few months, the woman continued to try to position herself higher than others on the leadership team by exaggerating her achievements and downplaying the accomplishments of others. She also went out of her way to take on more responsibilities so she would be an invaluable asset to the church. And she did, in fact, become that. She filled in gaps where there was a need and helped things run more efficiently.

However, a few months later, the senior pastor welcome a husband-and-wife pastoral team to our church leadership team. They had been pastors for more than 20 years in another county but moved to the area to help our church. Our senior pastor asked the wife to head up the women's ministry at the church when the church experienced a vacancy for that position. When the ambitious woman heard that the new pastor was asked to be the women's pastor, she quit the leadership team and she stopped attending the church all together. She probably thought she deserved the title of the Women's Ministry Pastor even though she wasn't ordained and had never been in a pastoral role.

The woman wasn't a bad person, and I don't think she was a wolf in sheep's clothing. But she did use manipulation and embellishment to wedge herself into positions. God knows how to guide pastors with placing the right people into positions within the church. God doesn't need our help to get us where we think we should be.

The behavior of this woman is quite common in churches. Most churches have volunteers and staff vying for positions and certain projects. Psalms 127:1 says, *"Unless the Lord builds the house, they labor in vain who build it; Unless the Lord guards the city, the watchman stays awake in vain."* This verse illustrates that it's necessary for God to be the one who makes the decisions in the church. If the Holy Spirit doesn't originate a program or lead a pastor to put a certain person in a position, it won't be successful. It won't bear the right kind of fruit unless it is originated by the Holy Spirit. With that in mind, why do people strive for positions? We need to stop trying to get leadership to notice us and trust God.

If we notice that a person is trying to manipulate a situation to get their way, we shouldn't act on it unless we are certain that it is at God's direction. God can handle overly ambitious people. Normally, He will cause a person to move aside without confrontations or the actions of senior leadership. God is able to displace someone with wrong motives. Even if it seems like people with wrong motives are excelling, God can still use them for a greater good. People with self-ish ambition can accomplish positive things. As well, if we have given financially to a ministry that has selfish ambition or greed, God will still honor our gifts and bless us. Or, if a young evangelist scheduled a service out of self-promotion motives, God can still use it to get people born again. God can use the good, the bad, and the ugly to bring about positive outcomes. Just because we don't see how God is handling self-promotion and manipulation, doesn't mean He isn't doing things behind the scenes. We shouldn't feel like we have a right to know how situations are being resolved by God. It isn't our business.

The Dream

Most churches are so desperate for volunteers, selfish ambition is rarely discussed from the pulpit. And as stated above, we understand that God can still use people in leadership with wrong motives to accomplish good. However, the higher the leadership position is, the more important it is to have a renewed mind without carnal motives. Senior leaders can do significant damage to a church and limit what God would like to accomplish if they have selfish ambitions.

I had a dream several years ago that I believe illustrates something God was showing me. In the dream, I was in a store and a few of us witnessed a woman steal a purse and run outside. We chased after her and I tackled her to the ground. Two pastors came over to assist me. She was a large and strong woman, so it was a struggle to pin her down and recover the stolen purse. As we wrestled with the woman, we prayed deliverance over her. We saw a bad spirit leave her body and then an amazing thing happened.

To date, I don't think that I have ever had such an incredible experience in a dream. The sky right above the woman opened up and rolled back like a scroll, and a sweet atmosphere came down from heaven. It was heaven – heaven on Earth. The new atmosphere came down and spread out as far as the eye could see. The air was thick and kind of sweet and was filled with joy and purity. The sky was tangible and contained the colors of a beautiful sunset. We started praising God and dancing. As we danced, we weren't constrained by gravity. As we jumped through the air, we could stay suspended in the air for dozens of yards before we actually landed back on the ground.

I believe the dream was symbolic. The big, strong woman represented the church. The church has stolen God's glory. Just as the woman had a wrong spirit, some leaders in the church have a wrong spirit, a spirit of selfish ambition. Some leaders in the church try to hold on to what doesn't belong to them. They want the attention on them. They want the honor. They want the glory. Too many church leaders carry selfish ambitions and don't even know it. They roll out their own agendas and label them as God's strategies.

The kingdom of God is not something to look forward to in the sweet by and by. Jesus said the kingdom of God is within us. The kingdom of God will manifest in our lives individually and corporately as we are set free from selfish ambition. The Lord's Prayer says, *"Your kingdom come, Your will be done on Earth as it is in heaven."* We, the church, can experience the kingdom of God here on Earth (before the rapture) as we purify our hearts and allow God to uproot things that don't belong in us.

Most people who carry selfish ambition don't see it. Like the woman in the dream, it's the normal atmosphere we live in. We are so accustomed to it that we don't recognize the spirit of selfish ambition. And, like in the dream, the kingdom of God won't manifest in our lives until we uproot it from the church.

Manifestations of Greed/Selfish Ambition

Selfishness

Greed and selfish ambition are byproducts of pride so, of course, they will have some of the same manifestations as pride. Selfishness can manifest when a greedy or ambitious person doesn't get their way. They may be stingy and want everything for themselves and/or they may believe they deserve more because they've earned it. When selfishness arises, the greedy and ambitious person won't view it as selfishness. They will have well thought out rationalizations and reasons of why they are entitled to more.

People can be selfish in their marriage, on their jobs, in their ministry, or with their friends. Selfish behavior can show up in dozens of ways, but it ultimately points back to putting oneself first.

Covetousness

Jesus said in Luke 12:15, *"Take heed and beware of covetousness, for one's life does not consist in the abundance of the things he possesses."*

James 3:13-18 says, *"Who is wise and understanding among you? Let him show by good conduct that his works are done in the meekness of wisdom. But if you have bitter envy and self-seeking in your hearts, do not boast and lie against the truth. This wisdom does not descend from above, but is earthly, sensual, demonic. For where envy and self-seeking exist, confusion and every evil thing will be there. But the wisdom that is from above is first pure, then peaceable, gentle, willing to yield, full of mercy and good fruit, without partiality and without hypocrisy. Now the fruit of righteousness is sown in peace by those who make peace."*

Truly, we shouldn't even think about the possessions of other people. It is not our business. If we envy what others have, it takes our peace and can invite evil into our lives.

Stress

Stress can be a manifestation of selfish ambition. Stress can be indication that we're trying to do something in our carnal nature rather than trusting God. When we walk in obedience to God, we have peace. Even when our circumstances are ugly, we have peace in our soul because consciously and subconsciously we know we are simply walking in obedience. We know God's got the thing figured out.

Without the peace of God, stress can become overwhelming and can take away the life of the carrier. Proverbs 1:19 says, *"So are the ways of everyone who is greedy for gain; it takes away the life of its owner."*

Our own greed, self-sufficiency, and selfish ambition can cause stress and can suck the life out of us. When we operate in stress, we operate in the flesh. We try to fix our problems and try to work harder. Some people become workaholics because they don't know how to deal with the stress. Proverbs 23:4 says, *"Do not overwork to be rich; because of your own understanding, cease!"* Working harder will not solve all your problems, just like becoming rich won't solve all your problems. We need to get the mind of Christ and listen to His instructions because peace comes with fulfilling His will.

Discontentment

We may not be totally stressed out, but we may have a general sense of discontentment. That discontentment can be a manifestation of greed and selfish ambition. Hebrews 13:5 says, *"Let your conduct be without covetousness; be content with such things as you have. For He Himself said, 'I will never leave you nor forsake you.'"*

Self-Promotion

When someone has selfish ambition, they usually take every opportunity possible to promote themselves. They tout their skills and achievements in hopes that those in power would place them in positions of authority or prestige. Within the church, we should never try to prove how spiritual, insightful, talented, or anointed we are. We should be humble and have a servant's heart. Matthew 20:26 says, *"Yet it shall not be so among you; but whoever desires to become great among you, let him be your servant."* We should have a servant's heart and allow God to judge the intents of our heart. 1 Peter 5:6 says, *"Therefore humble yourselves under the mighty hand of God, that He may exalt you in due time."*

In Philippians 1:15, Paul wrote, *"Some indeed preach Christ even from envy and strife, and some from good will. The former preach Christ from selfish ambition, not sincerely, supposing to add affliction to my chains."*

We don't need to showcase our ministry gifts or even mention our callings if we are called by God to preach. We just need to trust and obey and allow God to do the promoting. Psalm 75:6-7 says, *"For exaltation comes neither from the east nor the west nor from the south. But God is the Judge: He puts down one, and exalts another."*

Closing Thoughts

As you can see from this chapter, the Bible is full of references about greed and selfish ambition. The natural world applauds greed and ambition, however, God's kingdom labels it as carnal behavior. Truly, we need to seek first the kingdom of God and everything else that we are supposed to have will be added to us, as it says it Matthew 6:33.

Sixteen

Negative/Critical/ Judgmental

God alone is the judge. What is it within human nature that feels the need to criticize, rationalize, and compartmentalize the actions of others? The Bible makes it very clear we are not to judge. Matthew 7:1-2 says, *"Judge not, that you be not judged. For with what judgement you judge, you will be judged; and with the same measure you use, it will be measured back to you."* Do we understand what this verse is saying? It is saying that if we judge a person by assuming their intentions and not knowing all the details of the situations, others will do the same to us. This verse is like Biblical karma. We do not know other people's conscious and subconscious motives for the actions they take. We do not know if they are following the direction of the Holy Spirit, or if they are being influenced by demonic suggestions in their actions. We don't know if there are hidden emotional wounds in their subconscious mind that are driving their behaviors. Why would we make declarations about the actions of others that are not clearly good or evil? Obviously, there are times when the actions of others are clearly good or bad, but most of the behavior people criticize are actions where it isn't clearly known.

I am always surprised by the hypocrisy of people. When I hear people criticize others, I often shake my head and wonder how they have the nerve to open their mouth or post a comment on social media, when their own lives are a complete mess. Are they so blinded by their own pride that they can't see the ugliness in their own soul, that they think it is okay to call out other people?

The Pharisees brought a woman who was caught in the act of adultery to Jesus and asked Him to judge her. They wanted Jesus to approve stoning the woman to death. In John 8:7, Jesus responds to them saying, *"He who is without sin among you, let him throw a stone at her first."* We need to drop the rocks in our hands and examine our own life.

A soul iniquity of a critical spirit is usually a by-product of one of the other *diseases of the soul.* Someone with a root of pride can also have a critical spot in their subconscious mind. They may have a know-it-all demeaner so, of course, they will criticize any idea or project that they didn't originate. Someone with unforgiveness/offense will look for opportunities to criticize and judge the person that they hold in derision. Or it can be a byproduct of religious pride, rebellion, jealousy, prejudice, or fear.

While a critical spirit can be a byproduct of several different soul iniquities, one thing is for sure. People with a critical spirit have lots of pride. Their pride makes them think they have a right to judge others and it blinds them to their own delusional thinking.

Someone with a critical spirit may accumulate accurate information, but they could still have the wrong conclusions. People with a crucial heart tend to be negative people so their conclusions to situations will usually have a negative spin. What they perceive as fact in a situation may not be the total reality of it because their focus is wrong. For example, when the twelve spies scoped out the land that God had given them, ten of them brought back a negative report. (Numbers 13-14) But two of them brought back a positive report. The facts were correct from both the positive and negative spies – that the land was very fertile but there were giants occupying it. The pessimistic, critical spies only saw a negative outcome. Whereas the faith-filled, positive spies focused on how good the land was (flowing with milk and honey) and viewed the giants as a temporary problem.

Being Negative

We understand that most people are either negative or positive; they are either pessimistic or optimistic. The general consensus is that people are hard-wired to either be one or the other. It is true that some of the 16 different personality temperament types are more inclined towards one or the other. However, it isn't true that we are destined to be pessimistic or optimistic.

Pessimistic people usually focus on fear and as a result, their mind rehearses all the possible things that can go wrong. However, what we choose to meditate on is absolutely a choice. So being pessimistic is a choice. To stop the cycle of pessimism, we need to make a concerted effort to stop vocalizing all the negative thoughts that assail our minds and choose instead to focus on and talk about positive things. The glass doesn't have to be half empty. In fact, when we speak negatively, we curse ourselves and others. We empower dark forces and give permission to the devil to rob, steal, and destroy. Proverbs 18:21 *"Death and life are in the power of the tongue, and those who love it will eat its fruit."* When we speak negatively, we give demons ideas of how to harm us and those we are cursing. The kingdom of darkness may not have even thought through the negative scenarios that we just blurted out. And unfortunately, as this verse says, we eat the fruit of what we say.

When I was with Coldwell Banker Real Estate in the 90's, there was a man that sat in a cubicle near me. If you were to look at him, you would assume he was very successful. He looked the part. He dressed well, he had a friendly personality, and he seemed trustworthy. However, sitting so close to him, I heard his conversations. He was new to real estate, and he lacked experience. Because his confidence level was low, he kept sabotaging opportunities for success. He never asked potential clients for appointments. They were calling the office because they had an interest in a certain property, but he never suggested taking them to see the property they called about. He answered questions about the properties, but he assumed the people he spoke with were not ready, willing, or able to purchase a home. He shot down potential clients without even realizing what he was doing. He was so negative on the phone, it made me wonder why he even showed up at the office.

I left Coldwell Banker to start my own real estate brokerage, so I lost contact with him. About a year later, I ran into him. He was working at the Home Depot because he didn't make it in real estate. He ate the fruit of his words. He spoke weakness, lack, and failure and he got what he asked for.

Manifestation of Negative/Critical/Judgement Attitudes

Discerning

Many, if not most, of the Christians that consider themselves to be discerning are usually just critical. The Bible tells us to know those who labor among us. It instructs us to rightly divide the word of truth (1 Tim. 2:15). For some people, they think this verse give them permission to judge, critique, and dissect everything they hear someone say or see them do. A high percentage of critical people believe their soul iniquity is a spiritual gift. Being able to detect a person's faults or perceived faults is not a gift. Discerning a person's gifts, callings, and positive attributes is a genuine gift.

Jump to Conclusions

The tendency to jump to conclusions can be a manifestation of having a negative/critical/judgmental soul iniquity. The first reaction is to assume the worst. A woman that used to be a very good friend of mine comes to mind when I talk about this manifestation. Most people who knew her assumed she was an optimistic person. At church, she appeared to say faith-filled comments and didn't say negative things. However, just because she didn't say them, didn't mean she didn't think them. She at least had the good sense to *"speak life"* over situations instead of *"speaking death."* She knew Proverbs 18:21 that talks about life and death being in the power of the tongue.

However, whenever something unexpected happened, her first reaction was to assume the worst. She had a soul iniquity of fear. But the fact that her mind always assumed the worst demonstrated that she had a negative/critical/judgmental root as well. And not only did she jump to the wrong conclusion about situations, she also leapt to the wrong assumptions about people. She didn't openly criticize others in front of people but since we were very good friends, she shared her thoughts with me. I remember being very surprised on a few occasions when she spoke ill of good people. I had no idea those ugly thoughts were in her head. She made assumptions about the motives and actions of others that shocked me. I tried to defend the people by suggesting different motives but after a couple times of doing that, she stopped sharing her thoughts with me.

Being Pessimistic

As previously mentioned, I believe that someone who is always pessimistic in their responses to situations has a negative/critical/judgmental soul iniquity. There is a difference between observing a situation, analyzing the information, and forming a conclusion that something is bad and assuming everything is bad without evidence to back that viewpoint.

Some people believe that pessimistic people are smarter than optimistic people. They theorize that pessimistic people are more informed and more aware of possible outcomes to situations. Some intellectuals even view pessimism as a character strength.

Others theorize that pessimism and optimism in a person boils down to a person's self-esteem. If a person is confident and successful, they will have an optimistic outlook on life. Whereas those with pessimistic personalities will be doomed to failure because they won't strive for improvement.

From the spiritual side of things, a Christian should be optimistic. You can't have faith if you are not optimistic. Faith is believing what God says about situation instead of embracing fear, defeat, and failure. Hebrews 11:6 says, *"But without faith it is impossible to please Him, for he who comes to God must believe that He is, and that He is a rewarder of those who diligently seek Him."*

Discouragement

There can be several different causes for a person to get discouraged or go into depression. However, in a general sense, it is caused by their uncontrolled thought life. When a person is discouraged, they are meditating on negative thoughts. If there are positive words spoken to them, they chose to ignore those sentiments and embrace their negative thoughts.

The problem is that most people don't realize that a large percentage of their negative thoughts are not their thoughts. Most people don't have the discernment to know that demonic suggestions masquerading as their thoughts are what causes them to get discouraged. For example, if you misunderstood a situation at work and said something that made you look stupid, that demon will hound your mind with thoughts of how stupid you are. That little imp can convince you that everyone thinks you are dumb, and you are a laughingstock at the office. You overreact to a situation that most of your co-workers didn't give a second thought to.

2 Corinthians 2:3-5 says, *"For though we walk in the flesh, we do not war according to the flesh. For the weapons of our warfare are not carnal but mighty in God for pulling down strongholds, casting down arguments and every high thing that exalts itself against the knowledge of God, bringing every thought into captivity to the obedience of Christ."*

By paying attention to the thoughts that cross our minds, we are able to recognize which thoughts are positive and which are negative, which thoughts are optimistic, and which are pessimistic. We need a metaphoric screen door to our minds, so we don't let in the flies (wrong thoughts) of the devil. One of the names of the devil is "Beelzebub" which means "Lord of the Flies." Just like flies are annoying when they fly around us and try to land on us, so are the subtle negative whispers of the devil. They are spoken to us to bring discouragement, defeat, and strife. The demon assigned to us will try to get us focused on negative emotions and wrong viewpoints, so it is important to develop our discernment and arrest and cast down the thoughts that don't align with what God says.

Hypocrisy

None of us are perfect. All of us have areas in our heart that need to be renewed. I think it is interesting that we put degrees on sin. We may point to a person's sexual sin and treat that person like a leper. We may even go so far as the warn others not to associate with them. We sit on our moral, pious pedestal and judge them, when we don't even recognize the wickedness of our own heart. We convince ourselves that we are keeping ourselves holy when we are breaking God's heart.

We, as believers, need to be Jesus' hands and feet on Earth today. We need to have the compassion and mercy that He has. We need to love others, regardless of their weaknesses and soul iniquities. We need to point them to the cross, where they receive mercy for their *diseases of the soul* the same way we receive mercy for our pride and critical heart.

There is something within human nature that makes us feel like our sins aren't as bad as other peoples. It is all sin in God's eyes. We need to stop being hypocritical by condemning others when we have issues that we need to work on.

Closing Thoughts

This chapter may have surprised some people. Those that have a pessimistic personality most likely never considered it to be a bad thing, and certainly didn't consider the possibility that it was a soul iniquity.

Constantly being negative is a choice. We can choose the thoughts we rehearse in our mind. Remember what Luke 6:45 says. The verse reads, *"A good man out of the good treasure of his heart brings forth good; and an evil man out of the evil treasure of his heart brings forth evil. For out of the abundance of the heart the mouth speaks."* What we say is a reflection of the thoughts we entertain. Every time a negative comment leaves our mouth, we should cancel it, repent, and replace it with a positive statement. We can do the same with the thoughts that cross our minds. We can cast them down, so they don't erect strongholds of wrong thinking in our subconscious programming.

I do want to make one point. While we are not to say critical and judgmental things about other people, that doesn't mean that everyone is supposed to be our best friend. Psalms 1:1-3 says, *"Blessed is the man who walks not in the counsel of the ungodly, nor stands in the path of sinners, nor sits in the seat of the scornful; But his delight is in the law of the Lord, and in His law he meditates day and night. He shall be like a tree planted by the rivers of water, that brings forth its fruit in its season, whose leaf also shall not wither; and whatever he does shall prosper."* This passage tells us that our close circle of friends and business associates should be godly people. When we are constantly around negative or ungodly folks, their ugly attitudes and actions can rub off on us and weaken our godly walk. However, when we spend time with good people, their good traits rub off on us and we will be more successful.

All of us are a work in progress. We can make huge improvements in our life if we are mindful of the negativity that comes out of our mouth, and we are aware of the thoughts we entertain.

Seventeen

Spots and Wrinkles

Pastors and theologians may have differing opinions on what the term "spots and wrinkles" represents. And truly that is the beauty of the word of God being living and powerful, as it talks about in Hebrews 4:12. The Holy Spirit can highlight a scripture to one person to give them a revelation and can highlight it to another believer in a different way to bring a revelation to them. With that said, when I talk about *spots and wrinkles* in this section, understand that this is how the Holy Spirit has illuminated the term to me. I, in no way, deem it as the only interpretation of the term.

I believe our spots are our *diseases of the soul* as detailed in Chapter 3 and discussed throughout this book. Our wrinkles are our glitches, our scratches on the record, that cause us to repeat sabotaging behavior, as discussed in Chapter 4.

The term *"spot or wrinkle"* shows up in Ephesians 5:27. Paul is giving marriage advice and then he changes the perspective and starts telling husbands to treat their wives the way Jesus treats the church. Ephesians 5:25-27 reads, *"Husbands, love your wives, just as Christ loved the church and gave Himself for her (26) that He might sanctify and cleanse her with the washing of the word, (27) that He might present her to Himself a glorious church, not having spot or wrinkle or any such thing, but she should be holy and without blemish."*

The imagery suggests that the church is like a bride that is wearing a white wedding dress. She is beautifully adorned, and her gown is without spot, wrinkle, or blemish. Special attention has been given to it and it has been prepared for the special day when Jesus comes for His bride. Before Jesus comes for the church (the rapture), the church will go through a sanctification season.

What does *sanctify* mean? Some definitions are: 1) to consecrate, bless, ordain, anoint, set apart, to make sacred. 2) to purify or free from sin, cleanse, redeem, absolve, to make acceptable.

Verse 26 uses the word *washing* and when *ing* is added to a verb, it changes the verb's time frame to present tense. Meaning, we don't just hear the word once and we are cleansed, but rather, it is a continuous process of washing. This is an important concept to understand for two reasons. 1) Our soul isn't automatically cleansed when we invite Jesus in our heart. Yes, we are a new spiritual being, but we still have junk in our conscious mind and subconscious mind. 2) The conscious mind is the gateway to the subconscious mind, so we have to feed our subconscious mind a steady diet of the word of God in order to grow spiritually and cleanse ugliness out of our inner man.

Revelation 19:7-9 says, *"Let us be glad and rejoice and give Him glory, for the marriage of the Lamb has come, and His wife has made herself ready. And to her it was granted to be arrayed in fine linen, clean and bright, for the fine linen is the righteous acts of the saints. Then he said to me, "Write: 'Blessed are those who are called to the marriage supper of the Lamb!'" And he said to me, "These are the true sayings of God."*

This passage talks about the *Bride of Christ* as well. The *Marriage Supper of the Lamb* speaks of the union between the church (the bride) and Jesus (the groom) which will happen when Jesus returns to gather the church. It says, *"His wife has made herself ready."* Most Bible scholars would agree that this means that prior to Jesus' return, there will be a purification and sanctification of the church.

Notice this verse says, *"for the fine linen is the righteous acts of the saints."* This verse also validates the theory that *spots and wrinkles* refers the junk in our subconscious mind since our behaviors are driven from there. Our actions reflect what is in our heart. I believe this section of the verse is implying that fine linen is symbolic of our sanctified hearts and when we are sanctified, we will carry out *"righteous acts"* which are the assignments God gives His end-time warriors.

As mentioned in Chapter Two, 1 Thessalonians 5:23 says, *"Now may the God peace Himself sanctify you completely; and may your whole spirit, soul and body be preserved blameless at the coming of the Lord Jesus Christ."* Like the bride of Christ verses, this verse also tells us that our spirit, soul, and body need to be sanctified prior to the *"coming of the Lord Jesus Christ."* When it uses the word *spirit* in this verse, I believe it is talking about our subconscious mind because our spirit where the Holy Spirit resides doesn't require sanctification. When it uses the word *body* in this verse, I believe that references our carnal, Adamic, flesh nature that can corrupt our physical bodies if we are living a sinful lifestyle. The verse sounds like a prayer or blessing. It is asking the God of peace Himself to sanctify us. This tells us that when it comes to our sanctification process and renewing our minds, it isn't all on us. God Himself will help us. Praise God.

Certainly, with all the geopolitical events that have taken place in the last couple of years, it would appear that Jesus' return is soon. And if that is the case, doesn't it make sense that the Holy Spirit will be pouring out revelation knowledge on how to recognize our *spots and wrinkles* so we can sanctify ourselves?

We are entering a season where God will use this teaching and teachings from others to help the Church prepare for Jesus' return. There are end-time assignments God will be authorizing that will require pure motives so soul cleansing is necessary. We can't repent of iniquities that we don't recognize within ourselves. This book helps the reader understand the different soul iniquities so we can surrender those areas to God and take measures to uproot them.

The Time Is Now

There is a sense of urgency to seek God and allow Him to show us which soul iniquities we have. We need to not only acknowledge which ones we have; we need to also actively take measures to uproot them. The time is now for two reasons:

1) Oil Takes Time

It's important to not procrastinate our soul iniquities. Remember the parable of the ten virgins in Matthew 25:1-13? Five of them weren't ready when the bridegroom arrived. When they found out the groom was coming, they left to get more oil. The bridegroom came while they were gone, and they missed their opportunity because they assumed they had more time.

Likewise, we may assume we will have time later to work on our soul weaknesses. However, uprooting iniquities can happen in stages or layers, like pealing an onion. New layers of understanding may come after a previous layer has been recognized and dealt with. There may be memories and insights with each layer. Some emotional wounds or wrong mind-sets may be buried in nooks and crannies of our heart, so it may take some time to be consciously aware of them. The virgins that didn't have enough oil in their lamps didn't consider the amount of time it would take for them to get oil. Similarly, working on our soul iniquities may take more time than we anticipate.

There are some nuances in this parable that I believe the Holy Spirit wants us to recognize. At the end of the parable, in verse 13, it says, *"Watch therefore, for you know neither the day nor the hour in which the Son of Man is coming."* Verse 13 tells us that this parable is talking about Jesus' return. The bridegroom is Jesus and the virgins are the church. In the parable, five virgins were ready and five weren't, meaning half of the church was ready and the other half wasn't.

Five of virgins didn't have enough oil. I believe the oil in this parable represents anointing. In fact, the word *anoint* literally means to pour or smear oil. There can be the type of anointing that flows through us as we are speaking. Or there can be an anointing that God graces us with to perform certain tasks. The five virgins that didn't have oil symbolize Christians that don't have an anointing in their life. They haven't died to their own flesh nature enough for the Holy Spirit to shine bright through them.

Whereas the virgins that had oil are those who have renewed their minds to the word of God. They have spent time with God and have actively endeavored to recognize their hidden sins of the heart. They have contended with their carnal nature and have tried to correct wrong heart attitudes and fleshly behaviors. The anointing of the Holy Spirit can flow through them more freely because their *spots and wrinkles* in their subconscious mind have been recognized and tackled.

These five virgins have gone through a sanctification process. I think it is interesting that if you look at the fifth paragraph of this chapter, you will see that one of the words used in the definition of "sanctify" is "anoint." The church's sanctification process is an anointing process!

Actively working on purifying our hearts will cause the anointing to flow through us when we speak, whether that be from a pulpit, to our friends at lunch, or in the line at the grocery store. We can also have an anointing in us for specific tasks. The Bible tells us that Daniel and Joseph both had an excellent spirit (Daniel 6:3 and Gen. 50:20-21). I believe that means there weren't strongholds of iniquity in their subconscious minds. God used Daniel and Joseph to carry out specific assignments. God wants us to be like Daniel and Joseph. He wants us to be spiritually equipped to carry out assignments that God will give us or has given us that will be activated in God's strategic timing.

I love the reference to lamps in this parable. Lamps in Jesus' day weren't encased in glass. Lanterns didn't have their flames protected by glass until the 1500's. However, if we visualize a lantern with mud smeared all over the glass, we will see that the flame that should be lighting up a room, is blocked by the mud. That is how it is with the carnality in our soul, it blocks the Holy Spirit from fully shining through us.

Psalm 119:105 says, *"Your word is a lamp to my feet and a light to my path."* When we have God's word planted in our conscious mind and subconscious mind, our level of discernment will be strong. We will know what path to take and the timing to move. When the Holy Spirit wants us to take an action, He can remind us of a scripture that will pertain to our situation to help lead us.

The virgins had to go get their oil which tells us they had to do something. Oil didn't just appear in their lamps. They had to take action to fill their lamps. Likewise, sanctification of our heart takes action on our part. We are not just zapped holy. Yes, forgiveness is instant but correcting behavior patterns can take time.

While not having strongholds in our subconscious mind does allow the Holy Spirit to flow through us more easily, it should be acknowledged that God can anoint people that aren't very sanctified. He will use people as He sees fit. Most of us have heard stories of powerful preachers that didn't have strong character traits or had areas of sin in their lives. God has a need to reach people with His message of hope, salvation, and deliverance and He will use flawed people to do it.

There are situations where God does require some of His ministers to correct a wrong behavior pattern, and if they don't, the anointing on their lives will lift. God's anointing for ministry can be conditional. I believe God warns His servants when there is an area of their life that He wants them to correct. If they continue in disobedience, God may cause the anointing on their ministry to leave. The removal of an anointing can be sudden, or it can lift over a period of time, if God gives them a season of grace.

God is still God; He can choose to use a person with diseases in their soul. The point is, we need to get the mud off our lamp. There needs to be less of us, so more of Him can shine through us.

2) The Window May Close

The second reason we shouldn't procrastinate dealing with our soul iniquities is we may not have the opportunity later. When God gives an assignment, those tasks often have a timeframe of obedience and if we miss that, we may miss our opportunity.

There are times in our lives when we are faced with crossroad decisions. If we take the wrong road at that intersection, when God is dealing with us, we will get further and further away. And we may not be able to find that intersection again. For example, even though I was raised in a Christian home, I was backslidden for almost ten years in my 20's. My heart felt far away from God. There were times that I wanted closeness with God, but I couldn't find it because I was too far gone on my own path. As discussed in the first chapter, our pride blinds us and hardens our heart. If we don't make the right decisions in the crossroad times of our life, our heart gets hardened, and it may be difficult for us to do it later.

Proverbs 1:28-33 says, *(28) "Then they will call on me, but I will not answer; they will seek me diligently, but they will not find me. (29) Because they hated knowledge and did not choose the fear of the Lord, (30) They would have none of my counsel and despised all my reproof, (31) Therefore they shall eat the fruit of their own way. And be filled to the full with their own fancies. (32) For the turning away of the simple will slay them, and the complacency of fools will destroy them; (33) But whoever listens to me will dwell safely, and will be secure, without fear of evil."*

It isn't that God won't hear us if we miss our season of obedience, but rather, our hearts will be too hard to hear His voice, so it will seem like God doesn't hear us. We have eaten the fruit of our own way and we are full of our own fancies. We can't hear or feel God because our pride has closed Him out.

So, I encourage you, if God has highlighted some soul iniquities that you need to work on, don't put it off. You may not have the opportunity to do it next week, next month, or next year.

Identifying and Acknowledging Our Soul Iniquities

How do we identity and acknowledge our soul iniquities? Most of this information in this segment was covered in Chapter 3, but I want to reiterate some specific points.

The first step in sanctifying our soul is recognizing our areas of weakness. Some people reading this may have known some or all of their iniquities prior to reading this book. While others discovered their *diseases of the soul* by reading some of the manifestations addressed in it. I am sure there are some folks that just thought that they were hard-wired a certain way without realizing that those behaviors were rooted in one of the twelve soul iniquities detailed in this book.

In addition to reading the difference manifestations of the soul iniquities, a way of identifying which ones you may have, is to ask God. You may be surprised if you go down the list and ask God about each one of them. It may shock you if He tells you that you have one that you didn't know you had. That is how I felt in 1995 when the Holy Spirit told me I had pride. I didn't see how it operated in my life, so it was hard to believe that I had it. However, after studying the subject, I learned that we all have pride. The amount or degree of pride can vary from person to person, and it would depend on their individual choices and thoughts they choose to embrace. When it comes to the other soul iniquities, ask God to reveal to you if you have a spot of it in your gut. Ask Him to remind you of past attitudes or actions that would demonstrate those behaviors.

You can also look at your family tree. Are there *generational curses* that tend to run in your family? I believe the percentage of people that carry *generational curses* of soul iniquities is huge. First, take an inventory and analyze which of the *diseases of the soul* tend to run in your family. And then consider your own thoughts and actions to see if that bent towards a specific iniquity is in you as well.

Next, review the past traumatic events in your life. Is it possible that a root of unforgiveness or fear was originated in your soul? If there is an area that you don't like to talk about or that you talk about too much, that can be clue that there is an emotional wound that isn't healed yet. Open wounds of the past are a breeding ground for soul iniquities. Just like in the natural, an open sore can invite infection if it isn't treated and protected correctly. The same is true with emotional wounds. If you keep a diary, go back and read it. Are there clues that you have been holding unforgiveness towards someone or towards yourself? Was there an event that scared you and left a mark of fear on your soul? What are your bad habits? Could they be manifestations of an iniquity? Examine your heart and search out possible weaknesses, wounds, and quirks.

And finally, ask God if you have a resident demon in your soul. I believe that more people than not have at least one demon in them. Some people have several demons. Some of those demons are active, trying to bring harm to their host, while others may lay dormant for years and only manifest in certain situations.

We live in a spirit world and most people are unaware that there are spiritual forces around us all the time. Science will even acknowledge that humans see and hear very little. Most people can't see spiritual forces. We can't hear radio frequencies. We can't see energies or auras around people. Our eyesight and hearing are limited. Even animals can see and hear things that humans can't see and hear. Are we really so arrogant to thinks that our natural eyes and ears see and hear everything?

Most people would agree that we have at least one guardian angel. (I have actually seen mine.) If God has assigned an angel to us, is it too difficult to imagine that the devil has assigned a demon to us?

The kingdom of darkness tries to kill, steal, and destroy and the easiest way to do that is for a demon to whisper negative thoughts to us. A demon will masquerade as our own negative self-talk and speak fear, discouragement, and strife, and in our ignorance, we embrace those thoughts. Most people don't *take every thought captive* (as it says in 2 Corinthians 2:5), so they think the demonic suggestions are their own thoughts.

Regardless of how soul iniquities start, we need to take measures to uproot them from our subconscious mind. There is no shame in having a *disease of the soul* that was originated from a *generational curse* or a demon. It doesn't matter how it got there; what matters is getting rid of it. Sometimes, it is helpful to know how a soul iniquity originated and other times it's not. I will explain more about that in the next segment.

After we have looked for our *spots* (soul iniquities), we should examine ourselves and attempt to find our *wrinkles* (scratch on the record, repeating, auto-response, sabotaging behaviors). Quite often, those auto-response behavior patterns are the manifestations of a specific soul iniquity. For example, it was mentioned earlier that I have a friend that always responds in anger when she is caught off guard in fear. That is an auto-response manifestation of a soul iniquity. However, there are other times that our glitches are not manifestations of a specific soul iniquity. The adult woman that cried crocodile tears when she didn't get her way with her family, is an example of that. In her case, a childhood behavior never got corrected so she carried it into her adult life. Glitches are neurological pathways that keeps taking us down the wrong thought or behavior patterns. As mentioned in chapter 4, our glitches are like coding errors on a computer. Those coding errors can be corrected, but they have to be discovered and specifically addressed before they can be re-programmed. It requires re-training our brain.

Identifying our soul weaknesses and wrong patterns is really half the battle. Simply being aware of them can stop some issues. However, most will require a purge.

The Purge

Once we have recognized that we have a *disease of the soul,* we need to repent of it. Repentance isn't a quick "forgive me" prayer. Repentance is a breaking of our pride. There is a humbling. Repentance has to be sincere and heart-felt. When we repent, it is like we take a sledgehammer and purposely crack the ice of our heart. Just like pride (metaphorically) causes a layer of ice between our conscious mind and our subconscious mind, repentance with humility, cracks that ice. Behaviors are driven from our subconscious mind, so we need to create cracks in our hard hearts in order for us to have true repentance.

As of this writing, there is a popular trend on social media that shows disgusting boils, cysts, and tumors being lanced and squeezed out. It isn't just popping pimples, these videos showcase all kinds of gross eliminations of puss, tumors, and cysts. Repentance is like these videos. If we just say a quick "forgive me" prayer, that is like taking an alcohol swab and quickly brushing over the top of the growth without penetrating the skin. However, if we break the ice of our heart, then it's like we lance the infected sore by cutting through the skin so we can reach the infection.

I know this is a crude analogy, but as mentioned in the *Diseases of the Soul* chapter, we need to see how ugly our own sin is. Soul iniquities are gross soul cancers.

In the videos, we see the boils, pimples, cysts, and tumors being lanced and the growths or infections are squeezed out. Sometimes the infection is a hard, grainy paste that comes out in small chunks. Other times, there is a combination of sludge, with thick lumps of infection, medium thickness of puss, and watery infection juices. And a third type of popping we see is where the doctor removes a semi-firm tumor that is attached to some connective tissue. With that type, the doctor has to make sure they properly cut away the connective tissue, so the tumor doesn't grow back.

After the cyst is removed, the doctor usually squirts an antibiotic cleansing liquid into the open sore to clean it out. That reminds me of the cleansing of the word of God. When we purge an issue in our heart, we follow it up by treating it with the washing of the Word. Ephesians 5:26 says, *"that He might sanctify and cleanse her with the washing of the word."*

The growths that are attached by connective tissue are the type that we need to understand what is at the core of it. What caused it? Was it a *generational curse*, a past wound, or a demon? Those types of *diseases of the soul* will need us to address the root cause of the infection, identify it, and properly dissect it, so it doesn't grow back.

Part of the repentance process is (metaphorically) squeezing and pulling; we are pulling up memories of how we have harmed others by our soul iniquities. We need to observe and understand the consequences of our words and actions and how they have hurt others and sabotaged our own lives. We need to take off the blinders of self-preservation that often causes us not to recognize how much our actions have wounded others and ourselves. We need to face the real truth, not our prideful, self-protective version of the truth.

We have to see the ugly side of an iniquity, otherwise, it is human nature to rationalize that our pet sins aren't that bad. We will take the posture that we haven't hurt anyone and no one else even knows about our iniquities. If we don't really believe our iniquities are bad, then we won't sincerely repent of them.

Tether Yourself

The word *tether* means to tie or attach a rope or chain to an animal. For example, a dog can be tethered to a long rope, so it stays in the yard. Of course, we are not animals, but it is good idea to give ourselves a short leash when it comes to our soul diseases. When we have an over-excited dog on a leash and he keeps pulling and trying to drag us, that is when we pull back on the leash to correct that behavior. That is what we do when our carnal behavior tries to pull at us and drag us in the direction it wants to go. We need to pull back on the leash and let it know we are in control, not our carnality. Any time we recognize a thought or action that could be a manifestation of a *disease of the soul* we have, we need to quickly recognize it and reign it in.

As children, many of us played tetherball which had an eight-foot pole with a six-foot long rope attached to the top of it and a ball was attached to the other end of the rope. Two players would try to hit the ball in opposite directions and the one that was able to get all the rope encircled around the pole would win the point. We would see the ball going in the wrong direction and we would need to swing at it to get the ball going in the right direction. When we keep ourselves on a short leash, we quickly jump into action to hit or correct an action that is going in the wrong direction.

There are some soul iniquities that can be corrected very easily. While there will be others that will be much more difficult. Some Issues, like pride, will be difficult and it will be in stages. We can squeeze out as much as we see, but if that infection is spread out, we aren't going to get all of it out with the first lump we squeeze.

I understand it seems hard, and the enemy of your soul would try to convince you that it isn't worth the trouble. He would say if a lump keeps growing back, why bother? Well, if you have seen the videos of the boils and cysts being popped, you would know that it is much better to get rid of as much as you can rather than leave it to fester and get bigger. It is better to have a one-inch lump that has grown back then a massive 4-inch mound that was left untreated. The bigger the infection is, the more dangerous it is to the body. Likewise, the bigger the soul iniquity is, the more damage it can cause to your life.

We need to remember and rehearse Psalm 103:1-4. It reads: *(1) Bless the Lord, O my soul; and all that is within me, bless His holy name! (2)*

Bless the Lord, O my soul, and forget not all His benefits; (3) Who forgives
all your iniquities, who heals all your diseases, who redeems your life from
destruction, who crowns you with lovingkindness and tender mercies."

God isn't a mean taskmaster. He doesn't demand perfection. He
understands the human condition. He comprehends the evils and iniquities that reside in the hearts of men. Just because the contents of this
book may be new to you doesn't mean that it is new to God. Humans
having pride and sinful motives in their hearts date back to the fall of
man. However, God tells us in this verse in Psalms that He forgives all
our iniquities, and He heals all our diseases. That means He can even
heal our *diseases of the soul.* He sees that we are on a path of destruction,
and He delivers us and even crowns us with lovingkindness and tender
mercies.

So even though we may not be instantly zapped perfect after we
repent of an area, we shouldn't give up. Remember, our conscious
mind is the gateway to our subconscious mind. When we recognize
a thought or behavior that isn't right, we stop and correct it, that is
how we change the neurological pathways in our brain. That is how
we re-write the computer code in our subconscious mind. By keeping
ourselves tethered to God's heart, we can easily recognize our carnal
behavior patterns. If we are tethered to God's ways, then we are walking in the spirit. Galatians 5:16 says, *"I say then: Walk in the spirit, and*
you will not fulfill the lusts of the flesh."

So not only does the Bible tell us that wrong behaviors can be
corrected, but neuroscience also tells us that as well. They both tell us
that old patterns of thoughts and behaviors can be broken, and new
patterns can be established. Neuroscience tells us that new neurological
pathways can be established in our brain by repeating that new thought
or behavior. We can create detours of thoughts and behaviors. At first,
that correct thought or behavior may seem like just a hiking path. But
after repeated action, it can become a four-lane highway in our brain
and become our new normal.

Everyone is Needed

Purifying our motives and correcting our wrong behaviors are important but we shouldn't wait until we feel holy before we step out and obey what God is telling us to do. Absolutely nothing would get done if we waited until we felt sanctified enough.

If we have several soul iniquities, it may be a good idea to prioritize which ones to focus on. I would recommend attacking pride and fear before the others. Pride is the main one because: 1) it hampers our discernment to hear from God, 2) it causes delusional thinking, and 3) there are traces of pride in all the other soul iniquities. The other soul diseases will be easier to diagnose and uproot if we battle pride first. Fear also needs to be tackled because that will give us the boldness to obey what God tells us to do. We are entering a season of hearing and obeying. We need to get rid of pride so we can hear correctly. And we need to get rid of fear, so we obey.

In a football analogy, all players need to be on the field. This isn't the season for some players to sit out on the bench. There are multiple plays happening at the same time. While the kingdom of darkness may be focusing on one scrimmage, God will be gaining ground and making touchdowns in other plays. The devil and his army of imps will be overwhelmed because God will be snapping several balls into play at once. God will have already assigned the quarterbacks, running backs, wide receivers, tight ends, and the offensive line. They will know their assignment and it will bring confusion to the camp of the enemy. Plays the enemy launches will end in defeat as balls are intercepted and more victories are won by God.

If you are alive in this time in history, it means that God has specific assignments for you. You are not meant to sit on the bench. Don't let your demons convince you that you aren't good enough or don't have anything to offer. This isn't about you and your talent or ability. It is about your willingness to hear and obey. That's it. The victory will be by God's hand, not yours. You are merely the vessel that allows God to use you. The Christians that relinquish the most pride and fear may be the ones that God uses in the larger assignments. Remember, this isn't about you. This is about your surrender to the purposes of God.

Your Plank

As you have read this book, you probably figured out which soul iniquities those closest to you have. I encourage you not to confront them and play flesh detective. Certainly, you can lend them this book, but telling them their iniquities may put a strain on the relationship especially if those iniquities are blind spots to them. If you do want to say something to your family and friends, I encourage you to be led by the Holy Spirit when you approach the subject.

It is always a good idea to focus on improving yourself before you attempt to point out the flaws of others. Remember what Matthew 7:5 say, *"Hypocrite! First remove the plank out of your own eye, and then you will see clearly to see the speck in your brother's eye."*

And truly, when we uproot degrees of pride out of our own heart, we will have better discernment to see the *diseases of the soul* in others and we will have the sensitivity to know if we are supposed to say anything or not. In the meantime, everyone should worry about themselves instead of pointing out the sins of others.

Closing Thoughts

Even though this book identifies soul iniquities that you may have, please remember that you are fearfully and wonderfully made (Psalm 139:14). There are way more good things about you, than bad things. You are chosen. You are one of God's very favorite kids. There is proof of that in the fact that He chose that you would be born in this generation. We are the generation that our forefathers looked to as being the blessed ones, the ones that will get to see the return of Christ. But before Jesus Christ comes for us, His bride, He will be manifested through us, His Church. We will do the works of Christ. Signs and wonders will flow through us. And the unique demonstrations that He will do through us will leave no question in the hearts of men, that God is real, and He alone deserves the glory.

The Church won't seek glory that belongs to God alone. Ministers that don't reign in their pride, will get replaced by nobodies that have made those heart corrections. There will be some well-known names but there will be no super stars. Every Christian has a specific purpose that God has designed just for them. Everyone is valuable and everyone is needed. God believes in you. Let us rise to the occasion with humility and boldness and watch God do amazing things through us. His kingdom come, His will be done.